Welcome
Extraterrestrial

THIS JOURNAL BELONGS TO:

CURRENT AGE:

LOCATION:

HOW TO USE THIS JOURNAL

BECOMING A LEADER REQUIRES DEDICATION

This journal was created as a tool to assist you in understanding the knowledge, qualities, and dedication required to become not only a leader, but the master of your own universe.

Each page of this journal was handcrafted to take you on a journey into the unknown preparing you for anything the world throws your way.

<u>There is simply no one like you.</u>
You are one of a kind and it's time to start acting like it.
The things you will achieve in this lifetime will leave you speechless.
The world is yours for the taking but <u>you</u> have to rise to the challenge.

I never said this journey would be easy,
but it's worth it!

Looking for some extra guidance and assistance?
Don't worry, we've got you covered.

Check us out online and make sure to follow us on social media.

Your journey awaits!

TheMoodyPool.com

LEADERSHIP QUALITIES

MASTER OF YOUR OWN UNIVERSE JOURNAL

AUTHENTICITY

YOU CAN NOT BECOME A LEADER IF YOU ARE NOT TRUE TO SELF. AUTHENTICITY MEANS YOU ARE HONEST WITH YOURSELF & WITH OTHERS.

SELF CONFIDENCE

IF YOU DON'T BELIEVE IN YOU, NOBODY WILL BELIEVE IN YOU. BEING CONFIDENT MEANS YOU'RE BRAVE ENOUGH TO TRY NEW THINGS AND TO KEEP GOING AFTER YOU MAKE A MISTAKE.

INTEGRITY

INTEGRITY IS DOING THE RIGHT THING, EVEN WHEN NO ONE IS LOOKING. INTEGRITY IS NOT JUST ABOUT HONESTY OR TRUST-WORTHINESS. INTEGRITY INVOLVES EVERY DECISION WE MAKE.

TEAMWORK

IN ORDER TO BE A LEADER, YOU MUST MASTER WORKING WITH OTHERS. THIS INCLUDES HAVING GOOD COMMUNICATION, PROBLEM SOLVING SKILLS, AND BEING ABLE TO FORGIVE OTHERS.

INITIATIVE

A LEADER IS ABLE TO SEE WHAT NEEDS TO BE DONE AND DECIDES TO DO IT ON THEIR OWN WITHOUT WAITING FOR SOMEONE TO TELL THEM TO DO WHAT THEY ALREADY KNOW NEEDS TO BE DONE.

LEADERS

M — LEARNS FROM MISTAKES

I — LOOKS FOR WAYS TO IMPROVE

N — NEVER GIVES UP ON THEMSELVES

D — DEDICATED TO THE PROCESS

S — USES SELF AWARENESS TO GROW

E — GIVES 100% EFFORT ON EVERY TASK

T — PUTS TALENTS TO USE

AUTHENTICITY

the quality
of being true
to yourself.

GETTING TO KNOW YOU

Who are you and what do you like to do?

NAME

GRADE

GENDER

FAVORITE FOOD

FAVORITE CHARACTER

FAVORITE MOVIE

FAVORITE THING ABOUT MYSELF

WHAT I LIKE TO DO FOR FUN

IF I HAD ONE WISH, WHAT WOULD IT BE

WHAT I WANT TO BE WHEN I GROW UP

IF I COULD CHANGE MY NAME, WHAT WOULD I CALL MYSELF?

SELF PORTRAIT

Look at yourself in the mirror and come back to draw how you look to yourself.

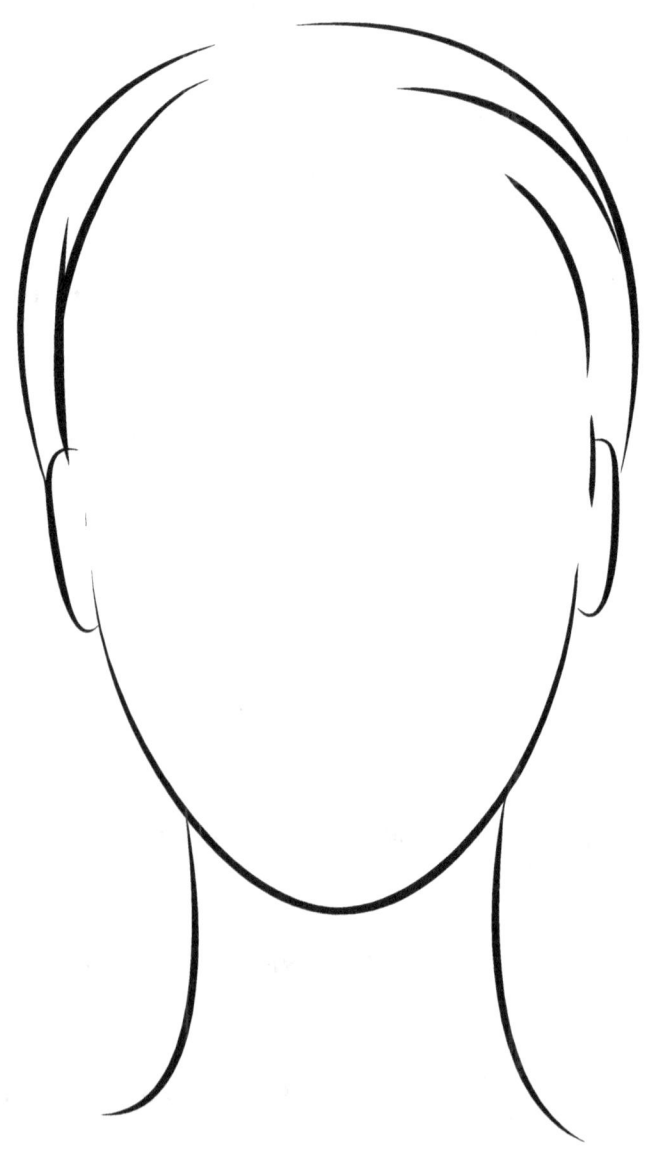

A-Z ABOUT ME

Pick a word to describe yourself for each letter

A
B
C
D
E
F
G
H
I
J
K
L
M

A-Z ABOUT ME

Pick a word to describe yourself for each letter

N
O
P
Q
R
S
T
U
V
W
X
Y
Z

BEING COMFORTABLE IN YOUR SKIN

Being comfortable in your skin means that you are comfortable just being you. You may not have the same hair texture as a classmate or the same clothes as a friend- but the things you do have make you special.

IN WHAT WAYS AM I DIFFERENT FROM OTHERS?

HOW DO I ACCEPT MY DIFFERENCES?

GOALS

Setting goals is a key practice that can benefit anyone with a dream or a vision for their future. In order to become the master of your own universe, you've got to start setting goals!

HOBBIES	FITNESS

HOME

FAMILY MEMBERS	FRIENDS

SCHOOL

PLACES I'VE TRAVELED

Color in the places you've traveled to. Haven't been many places? Use this as motivation to get out and see the world!

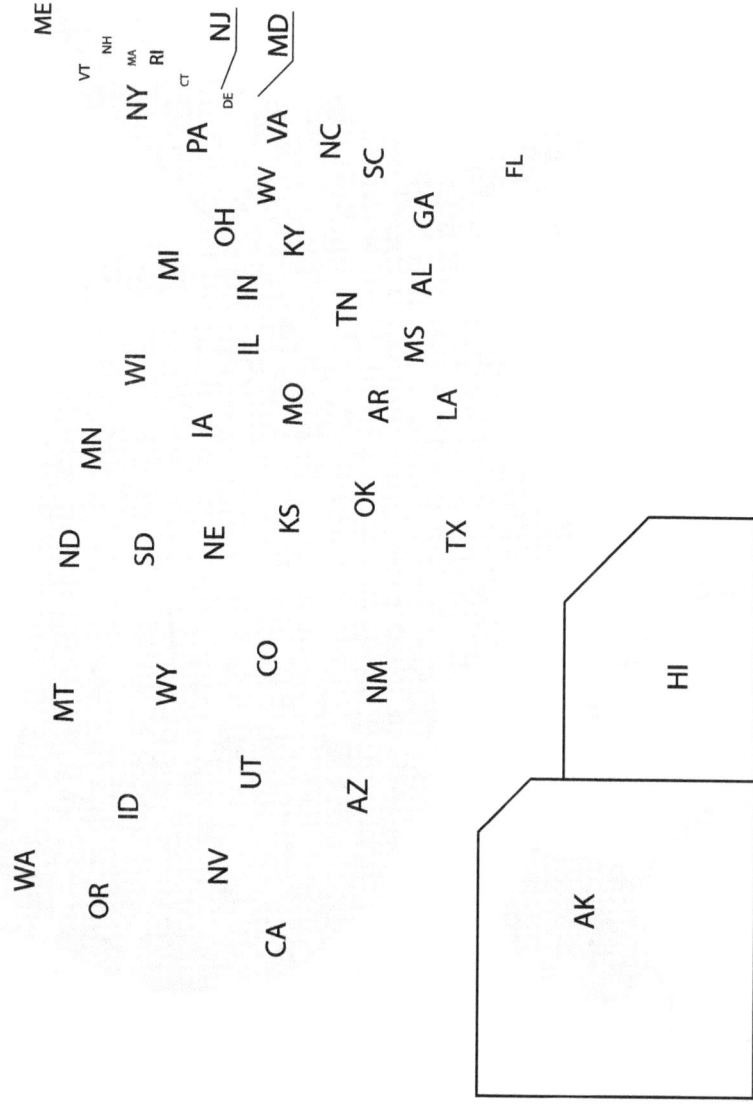

BOOKSHELF

What books have you read recently? Haven't read any, now's your chance.

QUOTES TO REMEMBER

There are hidden gems all around us, especially in the things people tell us.

Speaker: _____ Time: _____
Location: _____
Quote: _____
_____

Speaker: _____ Time: _____
Location: _____
Quote: _____
_____

Speaker: _____ Time: _____
Location: _____
Quote: _____
_____

Speaker: _____ Time: _____
Location: _____
Quote: _____
_____

SELF CONFIDENCE

the quality
of being confident
in who you are.

NEGATIVE VOICE

You know that voice in your head
that always has something bad or negative
to say about everything.
Draw this person and give them a name.

Name: _____

Next time this person has something to say,
simply tell that voice
"I know who you are and this is not the time."

WORRY LOG

**What things do you worry about?
List them in the bubbles below
(don't rush to fill out, come back throughout your
journey and leave your worries on the paper.)**

POSITIVE AFFIRMATIONS

I AM SAFE

I AM LOVED

I AM UNIQUE

I AM KIND

I AM SMART

I AM CAPABLE

COMPLIMENTS

Think about how people view you.
Use this space to write down five nice things
people say about you.

1. _____

2. _____

3. _____

4. _____

5. _____

WINS LIST

Did you ace a test, manage not to loose your house key, or kept your room clean everyday this week? Use this space to write down your wins.
(Fill in over the next 6 months)

POSITIVE SELF TALK

How you talk to yourself makes you feel more confident and boosts your self esteem.

WHAT FIVE WORDS DO YOU THINK BEST DESCRIBE YOU?

I FEEL MOST PROUD OF MYSELF WHEN

WHAT DO YOU KNOW HOW TO DO THAT YOU CAN TEACH OTHERS?

MY BEST PERSONALITY TRAIT IS

MY FAMILY ADMIRES ME FOR MY

LETTER TO YOURSELF

Use this space to write a letter about how you are going to change the world.

....
....
....
....
....
....
....
....
....
....
....

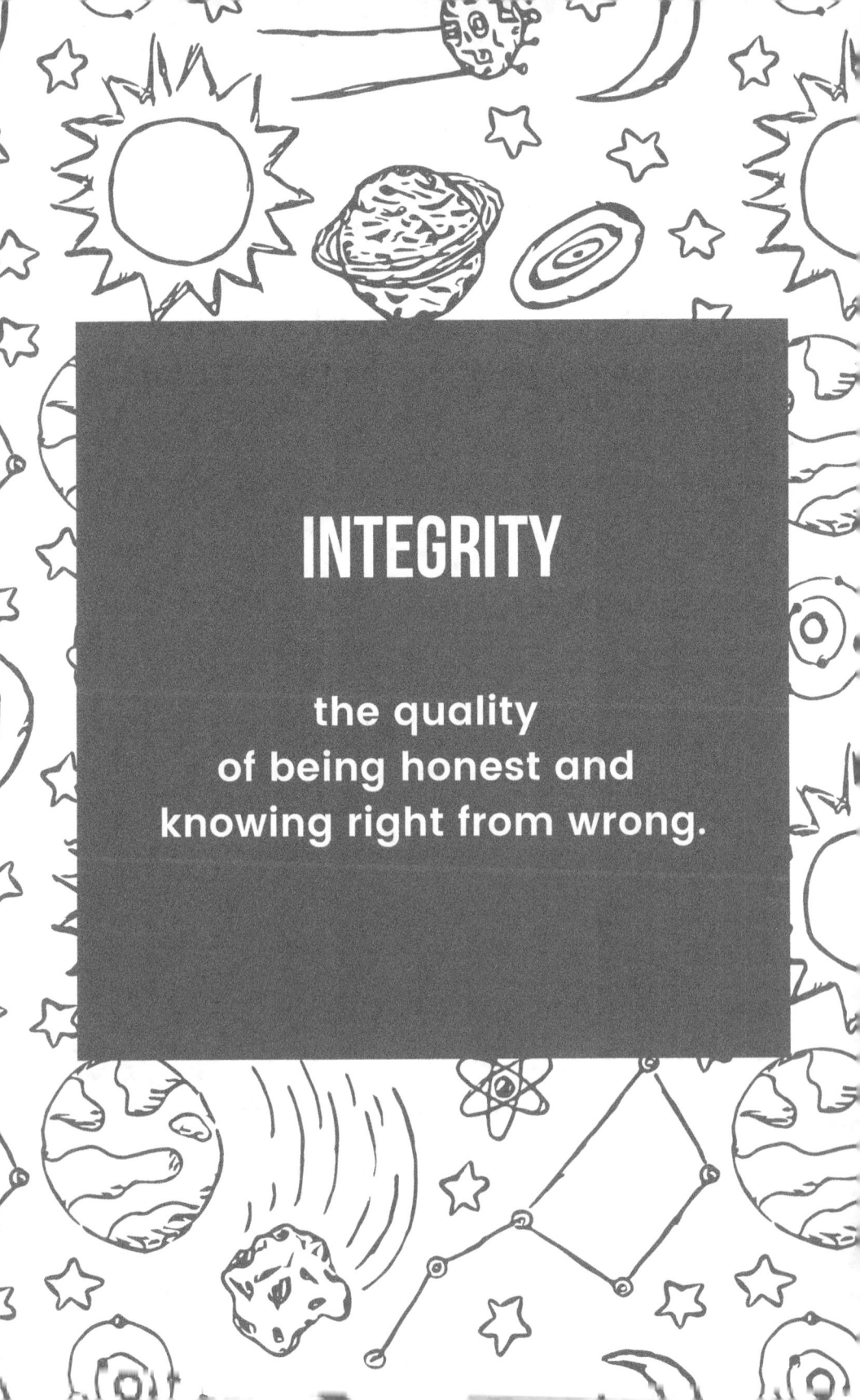

INTEGRITY

the quality
of being honest and
knowing right from wrong.

BEING A LEADER AT HOME

IS
- helpful
- respectful
- responsible
- kind
- friendly

IS NOT
- impatient
- mean
- selfish
- pushy
- a bully

SAYS
- please/thank you
- excuse me
- can I help you
- can I have. . .
- i'm sorry

DOES
- tries his/her best
- ask doesn't take
- listens carefully
- shares
- offers to help without being asked

BEING A LEADER AT SCHOOL

IS
- kind to everyone
- helpful
- respectful
- friendly
- patient

IS NOT
- a gossiper
- a bully
- a class clown
- an interrupter
- a distraction

SAYS
- please/thank you
- you are welcome
- how are you
- i'm sorry
- can you help me

DOES
- interact with classmates
- give more than they take
- ask permission
- raise hand to speak
- hold the door for others

SELF AWARENESS

Self-awareness is having an accurate understanding of ourselves.

My strengths	My weaknesses
....	....
....	....
....	....
....	....

MY EMOTIONS

How do your emotions make you feel?
Draw an emoji for each emotions and list how it makes you feel.

FRUSTRATED	JEALOUS	FRIGHTENED	EMBARRASSED

....
....
....

KNOWING THE DIFFERENCE

Leader vs Follower

Leader	Follower
Think for myself	Does what others do
Stands apart	Fits in with the crowd
Trustworthy	Can't be trusted
Empowers others	Makes fun of others
Solves problems	Creates problems

SELF CONTROL

The ability to stop and think before making a choice.

WRITE DOWN DIFFERENT THOUGHTS YOU HAVE IN YOUR HEAD ABOUT OTHERS (FOR EXAMPLE: FRIENDS, TEACHERS, CLASSMATES, FAMILY MEMBERS, ETC.)

```
┌─────────────────────────────────────────┐
│                                         │
│                                         │
│                                         │
│                                         │
└─────────────────────────────────────────┘
```

KEEP TO MYSELF   **SAY OUT LOUD**

THINGS THAT MAKE ME UPSET

**What things make you upset?
Write them in the bubbles below**

It's important to understand your "triggers" (what makes you upset) so you can work on not allowing them to have power over you.

NAVIGATING BAD DAYS

You will have bad days, we all do. Ask yourself these questions when dealing with bad days in order to find a way to keep pushing.

DO YOU NEED A HUG?

HAVE YOU SHOWERED TODAY?

HAVE YOU GOTTEN SOME FRESH AIR?

ARE YOU HYDRATED?

HAVE YOU EATEN IN THE PAST 3 HOURS?

HAVE YOU STRETCHED YOUR BODY?

HAVE YOU DANCED/SUNG TODAY?

HAVE YOU SAID SOMETHING NICE TO YOURSELF TODAY?

HAVE YOU SPENT TOO MUCH TIME ONLINE?

IN WHAT HEALTHY WAYS DO YOU DEAL WITH BAD DAYS?

HAPPNIESS

What things make you happy?
Fill this page with things that make you happy and come back to this page when you need a pick me up.

A sweet treat

Time with friends

My fav foods

THINGS THAT MAKE ME HAPPY

MINDFULNESS

Mindfulness is the process of accepting what is without trying to change it.

Let's practice responding to some situations we don't have control over.

A CLASSMATE STEALS YOUR FAVORITE PENCIL

YOUR FAVORITE TEACHER PASSES AWAY

YOU SPRAIN YOUR ANKLE AND CAN'T WALK FOR WEEKS

RESPECT

How can you practice showing respect?

In public
- Listening to your parents/adults
- Helping others
- Waiting your turn
- Showing kindness
- Giving eye contact

At Home
- Helping family members
- Cleaning up after yourself
- Doing your chores
- Taking initiative
- Taking care of pets

Outside
- Showing kindness to others
- Playing by the rules
- Not being too rough
- Being helpful
- Being aware of the little ones

In school
- Listening to your teacher
- Raising your hand before speaking
- Not making unnecessary comments
- Following the rules
- Being nice

KINDNESS JOURNAL

Being kind to others makes you happier, reduces stress, and improves self-esteem. (Fill this page in throughout your journey)

Kind things people did for me:	Kind things I did for others:
_____	_____
_____	_____
_____	_____
_____	_____
_____	_____
_____	_____
_____	_____
_____	_____

TEAM WORK

the quality
of working
well with others.

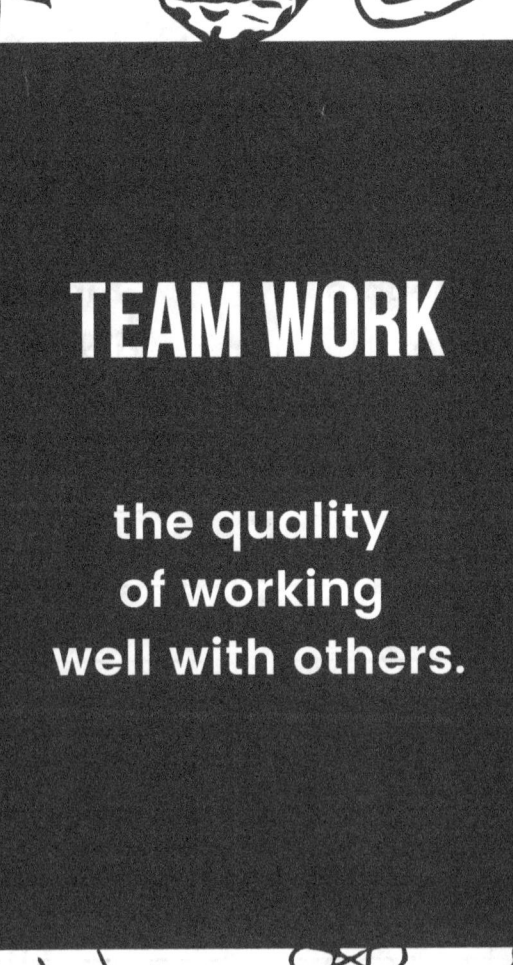

ACTIVE LISTENING

How do I actively listen?

- **SIT UP STRAIGHT**
- **DON'T INTERRUPT**
- **GIVE EYE CONTACT**
- **USE YOUR FACIAL EXPRESSIONS TO SHOW YOU ARE LISTENING**
- **PAY ATTENTION (FOCUS ON WHAT THE SPEAKER IS SAYING)**

Bonus- Ask follow up questions

KNOWING THE DIFFERENCE

Tattling vs Telling

Tattling	Telling
Getting someone into trouble	Keeping someone safe
Unimportant	Important
Harmless	Dangerous
Mean-spirited	Leadership-minded
Can solve on your own	Need help from an adult

BOTHERED

When something is bothering you,
What do you do? What do you say?

Actions | Speak

Actions	Speak
I CAN WALK AWAY	STOP
COOL DOWN	NO. I DON'T LIKE THAT.
TALK TO SOMEONE ABOUT IT	I DON'T LIKE IT WHEN YOU _____
WRITE IT DOWN	I'M UPSET BECAUSE

QUALITIES OF A GREAT FRIEND

- Kind
- Supportive
- Trustworthy
- Honest
- Grateful

BULLYING

BULLYING IS UNWANTED AND AGGRESSIVE BEHAVIOR

VERBAL BULLYING

- name-calling
- making fun of
- threatening to cause harm

SOCIAL BULLYING

- spreading rumors about someone
- embarrassing someone in public

PHYSICAL BULLYING

- hitting/kicking/pinching
- spitting
- tripping/pushing
- taking or breaking someone's things

BULLYING

ONLINE BULLYING TAKES PLACE ON CELLPHONES AND COMPUTERS

CYBER BULLYING

- Imitating others online
- Excluding others online
- Stealing someone's passwords
- Setting up fake profiles pretending to be someone else
- Posting unkind messages or inappropriate images.
- Sharing someone's personal or embarrassing information online.
- Sending abusive or threatening text or email messages.
- Spreading rumors via email or posting on social media.

ACCEPTANCE

It's important to practice acceptance not only with self but with those who are different than we are.

Sometimes babies are born with disabilities and other times people develop disabilities later in life.

 **There's nothing wrong with people who have a disability**

We've all heard some unkind words used to describe someone's disability. These hurtful things are not OK and shouldn't be repeated.

Always ask, "Is there anything I can do to help?" this gives the other person an opportunity to say whether assistance would be appreciated.

There is still so much you have in common with those that are different than you are.

Be kind to everyone and choose your friends wisely!

RESPONSIBILITY

WHAT IS RESPONSIBILITY?

RESPONSIBILITY MEANS YOU DO THE THINGS YOU ARE SUPPOSED TO DO AND ACCEPT THE RESULTS OF YOUR ACTIONS

QUALITIES OF A RESPONSIBLE PERSON

TAKING INITIATIVE
TRUSTWORTHY
ACCOUNTABILE
DEPENDABLE

RESPONSIBILITY EXAMPLES	NON-RESPONSIBILITY EXAMPLES
CLEANING UP AFTER YOURSELF	LEAVING MESSES FOR OTHERS TO CLEAN UP
FINISHING TASKS WITHOUT BEING TOLD	LEAVING TASKS UNFINISHED
IGNORING DISTRACTIONS	FEEDING INTO DISTRACTIONS

WHAT CHANGES CAN I MAKE TO BE MORE RESPONSIBLE?

INITIATIVE

the quality
to act or take charge
before others do

THINGS I CAN CONTROL

You are more powerful than you think. There are so many things that you are in control of- remember you are the master of your own universe!

My actions	My words	Using my manners	My level of effort	How I respond
		My attitude		
Screen time	Good sleep	My goals	Who my friends are	My thoughts

THINGS I CAN'T CONTROL

There are a ton of things that we can't control in life. We must learn to accept the things that we cannot change and continue to focus on what we have control over in our lives.

The actions of others	The words of others	Mean spirited people	Others lack of effort	The weather
		How others respond		
What others think	Loosing people we love	Things I have to do	Past Mistakes	Being Sick

DREAM LOG

Dreams come from the same place
in your brain that your feelings come from,
so they can help us realize different things.
Keep a log of your dream below.

Date: _____
Dream: _____
_____
_____

Date: _____
Dream: _____
_____
_____

Date: _____
Dream: _____
_____
_____

Date: _____
Dream: _____
_____
_____

MAKING FRIENDS

It's important to build lasting friendships early on in life. Having trouble finding your friends, check out these helpful tips.

Focus on things you have in common like a favorite subject, TV show or book

Mix up your routine and talk to someone different or try a new hobby/sport where you can meet other people

Be a good listener and make sure you give the other person a chance to talk before jumping in with another question or comment!

Show an interest in others by asking them questions about things they're interested in or things that you might have in common.

Keep things light and fun. Show off your sense of humor.

Be kind by sharing positive things about others or break the ice with a genuine compliment.

GETTING ACTIVE

OVER THE NEXT COUPLE OF MONTHS,
KNOCK OUT SOME OF THESE TASKS

TASKS

- [ ] START A GAME OF KICKBALL
- [ ] DANCE AROUND THE HOUSE
- [ ] PLAY CATCH WITH A FRIEND
- [ ] JUMPING JACK CONTEST
- [ ] TAKE A WALK
- [ ] PRACTICE A HANDSTAND
- [ ] GO ROLLERSKATING
- [ ] CREATE AN OBSTACLE COURSE
- [ ] DO A SCAVENGER HUNT

HOW DID I FEEL?

WHAT DID I LEARN?

WHAT DID I GAIN?

BEING POSITIVE

Having a positive outlook on life can help you:

- BROADEN YOUR SENSE OF POSSIBILITY
- OPEN YOUR MIND
- ALLOW YOU TO BUILD NEW SKILLS

ACCEPTING CRITICISM

Being criticized is a part of life!
If you are able to digest and apply
the criticisms given to you,
it will help you improve.

WHEN YOU ACCEPT CRITICISM, YOU NEED TO:

- PRACTICE ACTIVE LISTENING
- MAKE EYE CONTACT
- BE RESPECTFUL
- EXPRESS UNDERSTANDING
- TAKE ACTION TO CORRECT YOUR BEHAVIOR

WHAT WERE YOU LAST CRITISIZED FOR?

WHAT WILL YOU DO DIFFERENTLY NEXT TIME?

PAVING YOUR OWN WAY

CHOOSE SOME TASKS THAT YOUR TEACHER OR PARENT ALWAYS DOES FOR YOU THAT YOU CAN DO YOURSELF. OVER THE NEXT FEW MONTHS, TAKE INITIATIVE TO COMPLETE THESE TASKS ON YOUR OWN.

TASKS

- ☐ ....
- ☐ ....
- ☐ ....
- ☐ ....
- ☐ ....
- ☐ ....
- ☐ ....
- ☐ ....
- ☐ ....

HOW DID I FEEL?

WHAT DID I LEARN?

WHAT DID I GAIN?

SELF IMPROVEMENT WORD SEARCH

```
L S E V I T A I T I N I
H E C O N F I D E N C E
T M A A S C R O S M I L
E A O D R T I R C I P B
A M N O E A I R T N F I
M D D S N R N R C D L S
W R I A N G S E T S H N
O U A O L L S H E E E O
R P O S I T I V I T Y P
K A O C T A G O N P R S
I N T E G R I T Y O T E
A U T H E N T I C O N R
```

LEADERSHIP **CONFIDENCE** **INITIATIVE**

MINDSET **INTEGRITY** **RESPONSIBILE**

AUTHENTIC **TEAMWORK** **POSITIVITY**

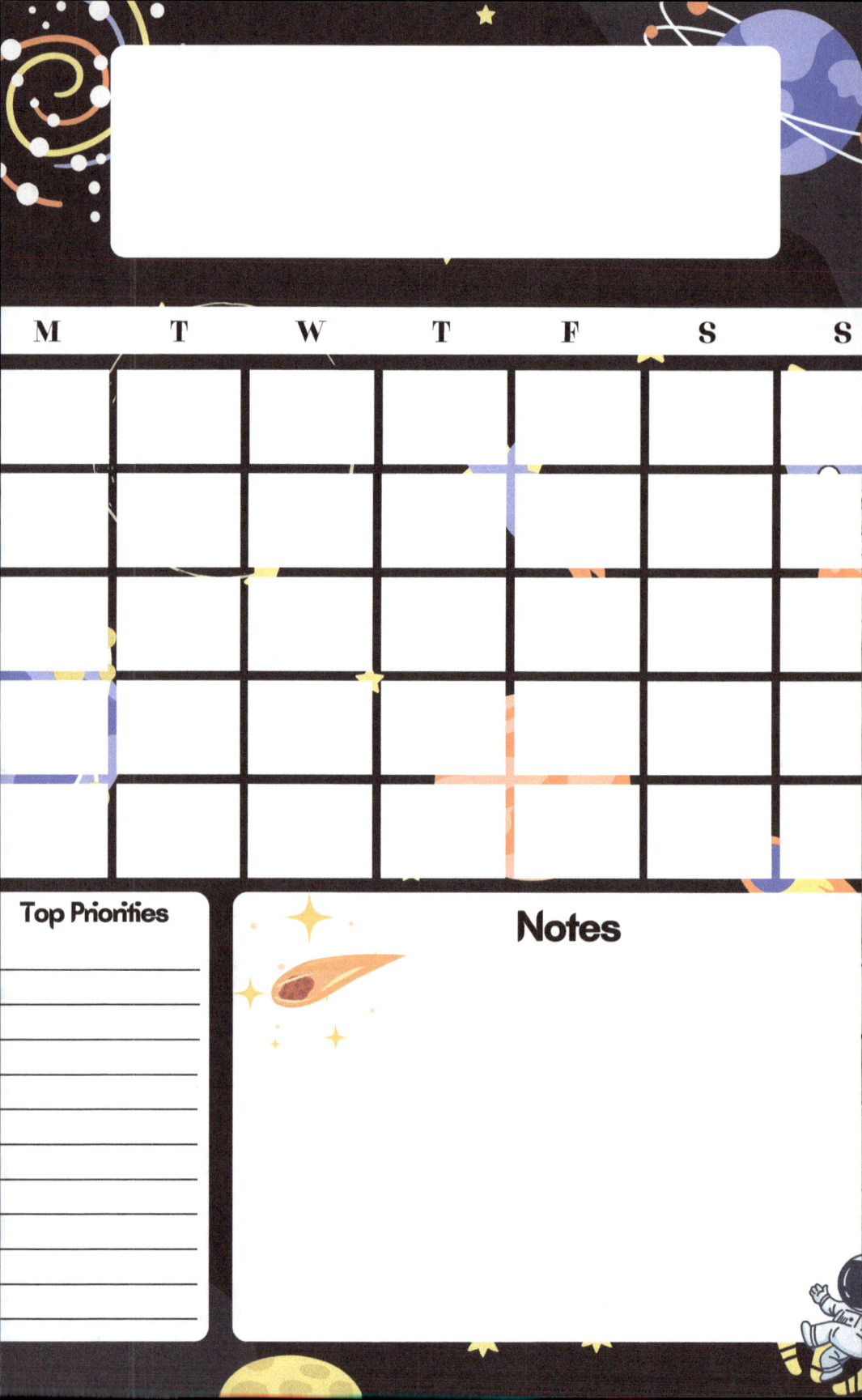

MONTHLY CHORE ASSIGNMENTS

What chores have your parents assigned you? (Grab a parent to help you fill out this page if you are not sure.)

DAILY CHORES

Kitchen
_____
_____
_____

Bathroom
_____
_____
_____

Living Room
_____
_____
_____

Bedroom
_____
_____
_____

WEEKLY CHORES

Kitchen
_____
_____
_____

Bathroom
_____
_____
_____

Living Room
_____
_____
_____

Bedroom
_____
_____
_____

EMOTIONS TRACKER

KEY

EVERY DAY FILL IN A SMALL PIECE OF THE PICTURE WITH THE COLOR LISTED FOR HOW YOU FELT TODAY

  HAPPY  EXCITED  WORRIED
 SAD  MAD  ANGRY

DAILY GRATITUDE LOG

WRITE DOWN 3 THINGS YOU ARE GRATEFUL FOR ON EACH LINE

1. ....
2. ....
3. ....
4. ....
5. ....
6. ....
7. ....
8. ....
9. ....
10. ....
11. ....
12. ....
13. ....
14. ....
15. ....
16. ....
17. ....
18. ....
19. ....
20. ....
21. ....
22. ....
23. ....
24. ....
25. ....
26. ....
27. ....
28. ....
29. ....
30. ....
31. ....

WEEKLY GOALS

WHAT ARE YOU PUTTING EFFORT IN TO GET ACCOMPLISHED THIS WEEK?

_____

_____

_____

_____

WHAT IS YOUR AFFIMATION FOR THE WEEK?

_____

RISING CHECKLIST

Morning Tasks   Mon   Tues   Wed   Thurs   Fri

_____

_____

_____

_____

_____

_____

_____

_____

Checklist SUGGESTIONS

wake up when alarm goes off	brush teeth	eat breakfast	make bed	get dressed
clean up	wash face	shoes/ jacket	put homework in backpack	brush hair
pack a lunch	feed the pet	clean out school folder	take vitamins/ medications	gather important school papers
clear dishes from breakfast	put pajamas in clothes hamper	make snack for school	double-check backpack	grab lunch and devices
use the bathroom	avoid technology	get school notes signed	hugs and kisses	turn off all the lights

WEEKLY CHORE TRACKER

WEEK OF _____

	M	T	W	T	F	S	S

	M	T	W	T	F	S	S

	M	T	W	T	F	S	S

Homework Tracker

Week: _____

Assignment	Time Spent	Due date	☑
1. _____	_____	_____	☐
2. _____	_____	_____	☐
3. _____	_____	_____	☐
4. _____	_____	_____	☐
5. _____	_____	_____	☐
6. _____	_____	_____	☐
7. _____	_____	_____	☐
8. _____	_____	_____	☐
9. _____	_____	_____	☐
10. _____	_____	_____	☐
11. _____	_____	_____	☐
12. _____	_____	_____	☐
13. _____	_____	_____	☐
14. _____	_____	_____	☐

Homework Tracker

Week: _____

Assignment	Time Spent	Due date	✓
1. _____	_____	_____	☐
2. _____	_____	_____	☐
3. _____	_____	_____	☐
4. _____	_____	_____	☐
5. _____	_____	_____	☐
6. _____	_____	_____	☐
7. _____	_____	_____	☐
8. _____	_____	_____	☐
9. _____	_____	_____	☐
10. _____	_____	_____	☐
11. _____	_____	_____	☐
12. _____	_____	_____	☐
13. _____	_____	_____	☐
14. _____	_____	_____	☐

EVENING CHECKLIST

Morning Tasks

	Mon	Tues	Wed	Thurs	Fri
_____	○	○	○	○	○
_____	○	○	○	○	○
_____	○	○	○	○	○
_____	○	○	○	○	○
_____	○	○	○	○	○
_____	○	○	○	○	○
_____	○	○	○	○	○
_____	○	○	○	○	○

Checklist SUGGESTIONS

read	listen to music	journal	recite affirmations	set goals
evening drink	take a bath/shower	unplug	clean up	pack bag
lay out uniform	make lunch	homework	chores	laundry
empty out lunch bag	feed pets	pick out clothes for the next day	charge devices	put on pajamas
brush teeth	go to bathroom	take vitamins/medications	double-check or set a wake-up alarm	go to sleep early

ACTIVITY TRACKER

WERE YOU ACTIVE TODAY?

	S	M	T	W	TH	F	S
WEEK 1							
WEEK 2							
WEEK 3							
WEEK 4							

IF NOT, WHAT ARE YOU WAITING FOR? GET OUTSIDE AND PLAY!

SLEEP TRACKER

HOW MANY HOURS OF SLEEP DID YOU GET LAST NIGHT?

	S	M	T	W	TH	F	S
Week 1							
Week 2							
Week 3							
Week 4							

IN ORDER TO GET 8 HOURS OF SLEEP, I NEED TO GO TO SLEEP BY

THIS WEEK

FAVORITE ACTIVITY

FAVORITE THING I LEARNED

FAVORITE MEAL

LEAST FAVORITE THING

WEEKLY GOALS

WHAT ARE YOU PUTTING EFFORT IN TO GET ACCOMPLISHED THIS WEEK?

_____

_____

_____

_____

WHAT IS YOUR AFFIMATION FOR THE WEEK?

_____

RISING CHECKLIST

Morning Tasks   Mon   Tues   Wed   Thurs   Fri

_____   ○   ○   ○   ○   ○
_____   ○   ○   ○   ○   ○
_____   ○   ○   ○   ○   ○
_____   ○   ○   ○   ○   ○
_____   ○   ○   ○   ○   ○
_____   ○   ○   ○   ○   ○
_____   ○   ○   ○   ○   ○
_____   ○   ○   ○   ○   ○

Checklist SUGGESTIONS

wake up when alarm goes off	brush teeth	eat breakfast	make bed	get dressed
clean up	wash face	shoes/ jacket	put homework in backpack	brush hair
pack a lunch	feed the pet	clean out school folder	take vitamins/ medications	gather important school papers
clear dishes from breakfast	put pajamas in clothes hamper	make snack for school	double-check backpack	grab lunch and devices
use the bathroom	avoid technology	get school notes signed	hugs and kisses	turn off all the lights

WEEKLY CHORE TRACKER

WEEK OF _____

	M	T	W	T	F	S	S

	M	T	W	T	F	S	S

	M	T	W	T	F	S	S

Homework Tracker

Week: _____

Assignment	Time Spent	Due date	✓
1. _____	_____	_____	☐
2. _____	_____	_____	☐
3. _____	_____	_____	☐
4. _____	_____	_____	☐
5. _____	_____	_____	☐
6. _____	_____	_____	☐
7. _____	_____	_____	☐
8. _____	_____	_____	☐
9. _____	_____	_____	☐
10. _____	_____	_____	☐
11. _____	_____	_____	☐
12. _____	_____	_____	☐
13. _____	_____	_____	☐
14. _____	_____	_____	☐

Homework Tracker

Week: _____

Assignment	Time Spent	Due date	✓
1. _____	_____	_____	☐
2. _____	_____	_____	☐
3. _____	_____	_____	☐
4. _____	_____	_____	☐
5. _____	_____	_____	☐
6. _____	_____	_____	☐
7. _____	_____	_____	☐
8. _____	_____	_____	☐
9. _____	_____	_____	☐
10. _____	_____	_____	☐
11. _____	_____	_____	☐
12. _____	_____	_____	☐
13. _____	_____	_____	☐
14. _____	_____	_____	☐

EVENING CHECKLIST

Morning Tasks

	Mon	Tues	Wed	Thurs	Fri
_____	○	○	○	○	○
_____	○	○	○	○	○
_____	○	○	○	○	○
_____	○	○	○	○	○
_____	○	○	○	○	○
_____	○	○	○	○	○
_____	○	○	○	○	○

Checklist SUGGESTIONS

read	listen to music	journal	recite affirmations	set goals
evening drink	take a bath/ shower	unplug	clean up	pack bag
lay out uniform	make lunch	homework	chores	laundry
empty out lunch bag	feed pets	pick out clothes for the next day	charge devices	put on pajamas
brush teeth	go to bathroom	take vitamins/ medications	double-check or set a wake-up alarm	go to sleep early

ACTIVITY TRACKER

WERE YOU ACTIVE TODAY?

	S	M	T	W	TH	F	S
WEEK 1							
WEEK 2							
WEEK 3							
WEEK 4							

IF NOT, WHAT ARE YOU WAITING FOR? GET OUTSIDE AND PLAY!

SLEEP TRACKER

HOW MANY HOURS OF SLEEP DID YOU GET LAST NIGHT?

	S	M	T	W	TH	F	S
Week 1							
Week 2							
Week 3							
Week 4							

IN ORDER TO GET 8 HOURS OF SLEEP, I NEED TO GO TO SLEEP BY

THIS WEEK

FAVORITE ACTIVITY

FAVORITE THING I LEARNED

FAVORITE MEAL

LEAST FAVORITE THING

WEEKLY GOALS

WHAT ARE YOU PUTTING EFFORT IN TO GET ACCOMPLISHED THIS WEEK?

_____

_____

_____

_____

WHAT IS YOUR AFFIMATION FOR THE WEEK?

_____

RISING CHECKLIST

Morning Tasks	Mon	Tues	Wed	Thurs	Fri
_____	○	○	○	○	○
_____	○	○	○	○	○
_____	○	○	○	○	○
_____	○	○	○	○	○
_____	○	○	○	○	○
_____	○	○	○	○	○
_____	○	○	○	○	○
_____	○	○	○	○	○

Checklist SUGGESTIONS

wake up when alarm goes off	brush teeth	eat breakfast	make bed	get dressed
clean up	wash face	shoes/ jacket	put homework in backpack	brush hair
pack a lunch	feed the pet	clean out school folder	take vitamins/ medications	gather important school papers
clear dishes from breakfast	put pajamas in clothes hamper	make snack for school	double-check backpack	grab lunch and devices
use the bathroom	avoid technology	get school notes signed	hugs and kisses	turn off all the lights

WEEKLY CHORE TRACKER

WEEK OF _____

	M	T	W	T	F	S	S

	M	T	W	T	F	S	S

	M	T	W	T	F	S	S

HOMEWORK TRACKER

Week: _____

Assignment	Time Spent	Due date	✓
1. _____	_____	_____	☐
2. _____	_____	_____	☐
3. _____	_____	_____	☐
4. _____	_____	_____	☐
5. _____	_____	_____	☐
6. _____	_____	_____	☐
7. _____	_____	_____	☐
8. _____	_____	_____	☐
9. _____	_____	_____	☐
10. _____	_____	_____	☐
11. _____	_____	_____	☐
12. _____	_____	_____	☐
13. _____	_____	_____	☐
14. _____	_____	_____	☐

Homework Tracker

Week:

Assignment	Time Spent	Due date	✓
1. _____	_____	_____	☐
2. _____	_____	_____	☐
3. _____	_____	_____	☐
4. _____	_____	_____	☐
5. _____	_____	_____	☐
6. _____	_____	_____	☐
7. _____	_____	_____	☐
8. _____	_____	_____	☐
9. _____	_____	_____	☐
10. _____	_____	_____	☐
11. _____	_____	_____	☐
12. _____	_____	_____	☐
13. _____	_____	_____	☐
14. _____	_____	_____	☐

EVENING CHECKLIST

Morning Tasks

	Mon	Tues	Wed	Thurs	Fri
_____	○	○	○	○	○
_____	○	○	○	○	○
_____	○	○	○	○	○
_____	○	○	○	○	○
_____	○	○	○	○	○
_____	○	○	○	○	○
_____	○	○	○	○	○
_____	○	○	○	○	○

Checklist SUGGESTIONS

read	listen to music	journal	recite affirmations	set goals
evening drink	take a bath/ shower	unplug	clean up	pack bag
lay out uniform	make lunch	homework	chores	laundry
empty out lunch bag	feed pets	pick out clothes for the next day	charge devices	put on pajamas
brush teeth	go to bathroom	take vitamins/ medications	double-check or set a wake-up alarm	go to sleep early

ACTIVITY TRACKER

WERE YOU ACTIVE TODAY?

	S	M	T	W	TH	F	S
WEEK 1							
WEEK 2							
WEEK 3							
WEEK 4							

IF NOT, WHAT ARE YOU WAITING FOR? GET OUTSIDE AND PLAY!

SLEEP TRACKER

HOW MANY HOURS OF SLEEP DID YOU GET LAST NIGHT?

	S	M	T	W	TH	F	S
Week 1							
Week 2							
Week 3							
Week 4							

IN ORDER TO GET 8 HOURS OF SLEEP, I NEED TO GO TO SLEEP BY

THIS WEEK

FAVORITE ACTIVITY

FAVORITE THING I LEARNED

FAVORITE MEAL

LEAST FAVORITE THING

WEEKLY GOALS

WHAT ARE YOU PUTTING EFFORT IN TO GET ACCOMPLISHED THIS WEEK?

_____
_____
_____
_____

WHAT IS YOUR AFFIMATION FOR THE WEEK?

_____

RISING CHECKLIST

Morning Tasks   Mon   Tues   Wed   Thurs   Fri

_____

_____

_____

_____

_____

_____

_____

_____

Checklist SUGGESTIONS

wake up when alarm goes off	brush teeth	eat breakfast	make bed	get dressed
clean up	wash face	shoes/ jacket	put homework in backpack	brush hair
pack a lunch	feed the pet	clean out school folder	take vitamins/ medications	gather important school papers
clear dishes from breakfast	put pajamas in clothes hamper	make snack for school	double-check backpack	grab lunch and devices
use the bathroom	avoid technology	get school notes signed	hugs and kisses	turn off all the lights

WEEKLY CHORE TRACKER

WEEK OF _____

	M	T	W	T	F	S	S

	M	T	W	T	F	S	S

	M	T	W	T	F	S	S

HOMEWORK TRACKER

Week: _____

Assignment	Time Spent	Due date	✓
1. _____	_____	_____	☐
2. _____	_____	_____	☐
3. _____	_____	_____	☐
4. _____	_____	_____	☐
5. _____	_____	_____	☐
6. _____	_____	_____	☐
7. _____	_____	_____	☐
8. _____	_____	_____	☐
9. _____	_____	_____	☐
10. _____	_____	_____	☐
11. _____	_____	_____	☐
12. _____	_____	_____	☐
13. _____	_____	_____	☐
14. _____	_____	_____	☐

Homework Tracker

Week: _____

Assignment	Time Spent	Due date	✓
1. _____	_____	_____	☐
2. _____	_____	_____	☐
3. _____	_____	_____	☐
4. _____	_____	_____	☐
5. _____	_____	_____	☐
6. _____	_____	_____	☐
7. _____	_____	_____	☐
8. _____	_____	_____	☐
9. _____	_____	_____	☐
10. _____	_____	_____	☐
11. _____	_____	_____	☐
12. _____	_____	_____	☐
13. _____	_____	_____	☐
14. _____	_____	_____	☐

EVENING CHECKLIST

Morning Tasks	Mon	Tues	Wed	Thurs	Fri
_____	○	○	○	○	○
_____	○	○	○	○	○
_____	○	○	○	○	○
_____	○	○	○	○	○
_____	○	○	○	○	○
_____	○	○	○	○	○
_____	○	○	○	○	○
_____	○	○	○	○	○

Checklist SUGGESTIONS

read	listen to music	journal	recite affirmations	set goals
evening drink	take a bath/ shower	unplug	clean up	pack bag
lay out uniform	make lunch	homework	chores	laundry
empty out lunch bag	feed pets	pick out clothes for the next day	charge devices	put on pajamas
brush teeth	go to bathroom	take vitamins/ medications	double-check or set a wake-up alarm	go to sleep early

ACTIVITY TRACKER

WERE YOU ACTIVE TODAY?

	S	M	T	W	TH	F	S
WEEK 1							
WEEK 2							
WEEK 3							
WEEK 4							

IF NOT, WHAT ARE YOU WAITING FOR? GET OUTSIDE AND PLAY!

SLEEP TRACKER

HOW MANY HOURS OF SLEEP DID YOU GET LAST NIGHT?

	S	M	T	W	TH	F	S
Week 1							
Week 2							
Week 3							
Week 4							

IN ORDER TO GET 8 HOURS OF SLEEP, I NEED TO GO TO SLEEP BY

THIS WEEK

FAVORITE ACTIVITY

FAVORITE THING I LEARNED

FAVORITE MEAL

LEAST FAVORITE THING

END OF THE MONTH RECAP

SMALL WINS
1. _____
2. _____
3. _____

BIG ACHIEVEMENTS
1. _____
2. _____
3. _____

HIGHLIGHTS
_____
_____
_____
_____

LESSONS I LEARNED
_____
_____
_____
_____

WHAT WORKED WELL FOR ME
_____
_____
_____
_____
_____
_____

WHAT I'LL STOP DOING
_____
_____
_____
_____
_____
_____

IMPROVEMENTS TO MAKE
_____
_____
_____
_____

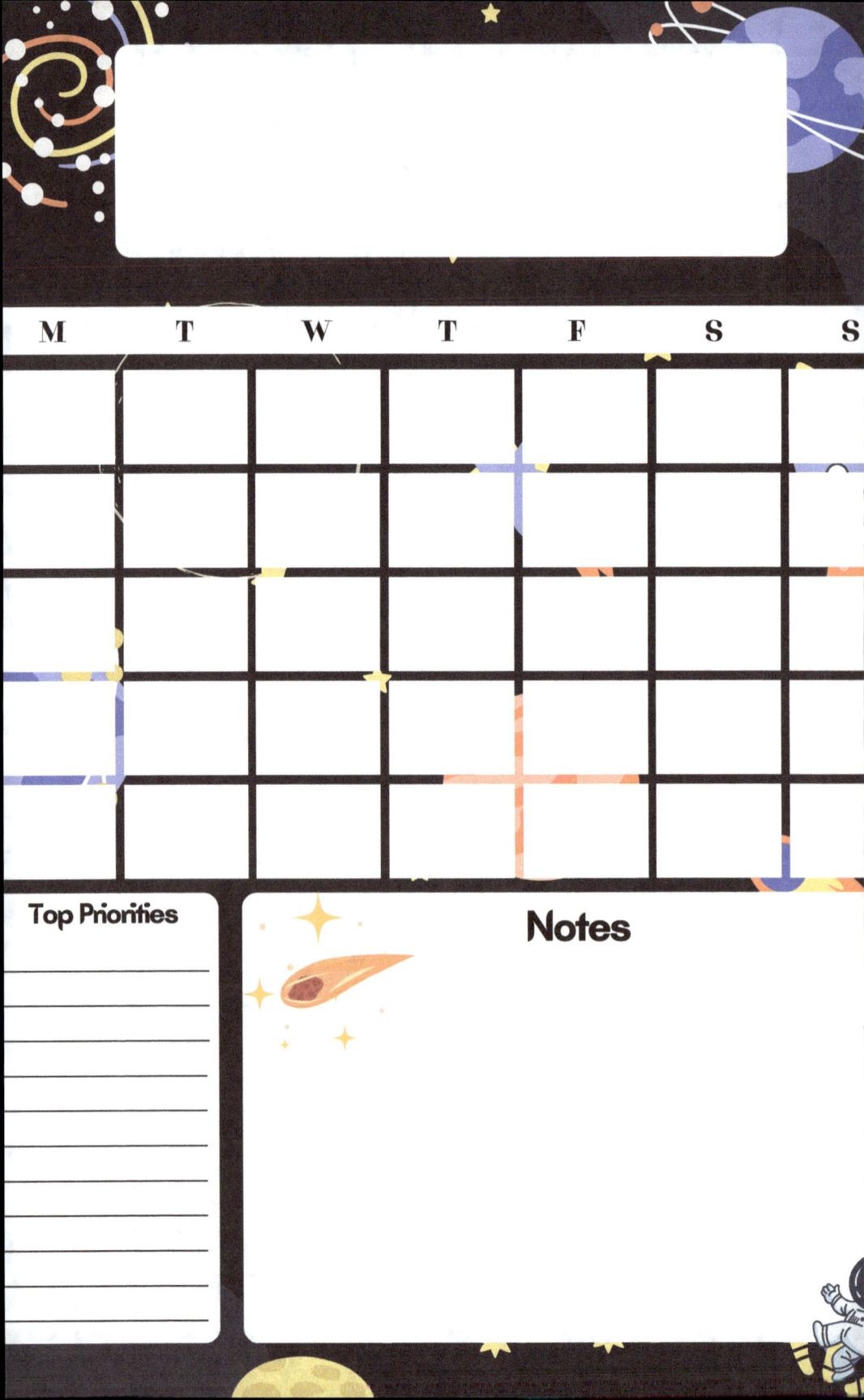

MONTHLY CHORE ASSIGNMENTS

What chores have your parents assigned you? (Grab a parent to help you fill out this page if you are not sure.)

DAILY CHORES

Kitchen
_____
_____
_____

Bathroom
_____
_____
_____

Living Room
_____
_____
_____

Bedroom
_____
_____
_____

WEEKLY CHORES

Kitchen
_____
_____
_____

Bathroom
_____
_____
_____

Living Room
_____
_____
_____

Bedroom
_____
_____
_____

EMOTIONS TRACKER

KEY

EVERY DAY FILL IN A SMALL PIECE OF THE PICTURE WITH THE COLOR LISTED FOR HOW YOU FELT TODAY

 HAPPY    EXCITED    WORRIED

 SAD    MAD    ANGRY

DAILY GRATITUDE LOG

WRITE DOWN 3 THINGS YOU ARE GRATEFUL FOR ON EACH LINE

1. ....
2. ....
3. ....
4. ....
5. ....
6. ....
7. ....
8. ....
9. ....
10. ....
11. ....
12. ....
13. ....
14. ....
15. ....
16. ....
17. ....
18. ....
19. ....
20. ....
21. ....
22. ....
23. ....
24. ....
25. ....
26. ....
27. ....
28. ....
29. ....
30. ....
31. ....

WEEKLY GOALS

WHAT ARE YOU PUTTING EFFORT IN TO GET ACCOMPLISHED THIS WEEK?

_____
_____
_____
_____

WHAT IS YOUR AFFIMATION FOR THE WEEK?

_____

RISING CHECKLIST

Morning Tasks   Mon   Tues   Wed   Thurs   Fri

_____

_____

_____

_____

_____

_____

_____

_____

Checklist SUGGESTIONS

wake up when alarm goes off	brush teeth	eat breakfast	make bed	get dressed
clean up	wash face	shoes/ jacket	put homework in backpack	brush hair
pack a lunch	feed the pet	clean out school folder	take vitamins/ medications	gather important school papers
clear dishes from breakfast	put pajamas in clothes hamper	make snack for school	double-check backpack	grab lunch and devices
use the bathroom	avoid technology	get school notes signed	hugs and kisses	turn off all the lights

WEEKLY CHORE TRACKER

WEEK OF _____

	M	T	W	T	F	S	S

	M	T	W	T	F	S	S

	M	T	W	T	F	S	S

HOMEWORK TRACKER

Week: _____

Assignment	Time Spent	Due date	✓
1. _____	_____	_____	☐
2. _____	_____	_____	☐
3. _____	_____	_____	☐
4. _____	_____	_____	☐
5. _____	_____	_____	☐
6. _____	_____	_____	☐
7. _____	_____	_____	☐
8. _____	_____	_____	☐
9. _____	_____	_____	☐
10. _____	_____	_____	☐
11. _____	_____	_____	☐
12. _____	_____	_____	☐
13. _____	_____	_____	☐
14. _____	_____	_____	☐

Homework Tracker

Week: _____

Assignment	Time Spent	Due date	✓
1. _____	_____	_____	☐
2. _____	_____	_____	☐
3. _____	_____	_____	☐
4. _____	_____	_____	☐
5. _____	_____	_____	☐
6. _____	_____	_____	☐
7. _____	_____	_____	☐
8. _____	_____	_____	☐
9. _____	_____	_____	☐
10. _____	_____	_____	☐
11. _____	_____	_____	☐
12. _____	_____	_____	☐
13. _____	_____	_____	☐
14. _____	_____	_____	☐

EVENING CHECKLIST

Morning Tasks | Mon | Tues | Wed | Thurs | Fri

_____
_____
_____
_____
_____
_____
_____

Checklist SUGGESTIONS

read	listen to music	journal	recite affirmations	set goals
evening drink	take a bath/ shower	unplug	clean up	pack bag
lay out uniform	make lunch	homework	chores	laundry
empty out lunch bag	feed pets	pick out clothes for the next day	charge devices	put on pajamas
brush teeth	go to bathroom	take vitamins/ medications	double-check or set a wake-up alarm	go to sleep early

ACTIVITY TRACKER

WERE YOU ACTIVE TODAY?

	S	M	T	W	TH	F	S
WEEK 1							
WEEK 2							
WEEK 3							
WEEK 4							

IF NOT, WHAT ARE YOU WAITING FOR? GET OUTSIDE AND PLAY!

SLEEP TRACKER

HOW MANY HOURS OF SLEEP DID YOU GET LAST NIGHT?

	S	M	T	W	TH	F	S
Week 1							
Week 2							
Week 3							
Week 4							

IN ORDER TO GET 8 HOURS OF SLEEP, I NEED TO GO TO SLEEP BY

THIS WEEK

FAVORITE ACTIVITY

FAVORITE THING I LEARNED

FAVORITE MEAL

LEAST FAVORITE THING

WEEKLY
GOALS

WHAT ARE YOU PUTTING EFFORT IN TO GET ACCOMPLISHED THIS WEEK?

_____
_____
_____
_____

WHAT IS YOUR AFFIMATION FOR THE WEEK?

_____

RISING CHECKLIST

Morning Tasks   Mon   Tues   Wed   Thurs   Fri

_____

_____

_____

_____

_____

_____

_____

_____

wake up when alarm goes off	brush teeth	eat breakfast	make bed	get dressed
clean up	wash face	shoes/ jacket	put homework in backpack	brush hair
pack a lunch	feed the pet	clean out school folder	take vitamins/ medications	gather important school papers
clear dishes from breakfast	put pajamas in clothes hamper	make snack for school	double-check backpack	grab lunch and devices
use the bathroom	avoid technology	get school notes signed	hugs and kisses	turn off all the lights

Checklist SUGGESTIONS

WEEKLY CHORE TRACKER

WEEK OF _____

	M	T	W	T	F	S	S

	M	T	W	T	F	S	S

	M	T	W	T	F	S	S

HOMEWORK TRACKER

Week: _____

Assignment	Time Spent	Due date	✓
1. _____	_____	_____	☐
2. _____	_____	_____	☐
3. _____	_____	_____	☐
4. _____	_____	_____	☐
5. _____	_____	_____	☐
6. _____	_____	_____	☐
7. _____	_____	_____	☐
8. _____	_____	_____	☐
9. _____	_____	_____	☐
10. _____	_____	_____	☐
11. _____	_____	_____	☐
12. _____	_____	_____	☐
13. _____	_____	_____	☐
14. _____	_____	_____	☐

Homework Tracker

Week: _____

Assignment	Time Spent	Due date	✓
1. _____	_____	_____	☐
2. _____	_____	_____	☐
3. _____	_____	_____	☐
4. _____	_____	_____	☐
5. _____	_____	_____	☐
6. _____	_____	_____	☐
7. _____	_____	_____	☐
8. _____	_____	_____	☐
9. _____	_____	_____	☐
10. _____	_____	_____	☐
11. _____	_____	_____	☐
12. _____	_____	_____	☐
13. _____	_____	_____	☐
14. _____	_____	_____	☐

EVENING CHECKLIST

Morning Tasks

	Mon	Tues	Wed	Thurs	Fri
_____	○	○	○	○	○
_____	○	○	○	○	○
_____	○	○	○	○	○
_____	○	○	○	○	○
_____	○	○	○	○	○
_____	○	○	○	○	○
_____	○	○	○	○	○
_____	○	○	○	○	○

Checklist SUGGESTIONS

read	listen to music	journal	recite affirmations	set goals
evening drink	take a bath/ shower	unplug	clean up	pack bag
lay out uniform	make lunch	homework	chores	laundry
empty out lunch bag	feed pets	pick out clothes for the next day	charge devices	put on pajamas
brush teeth	go to bathroom	take vitamins/ medications	double-check or set a wake-up alarm	go to sleep early

ACTIVITY TRACKER

WERE YOU ACTIVE TODAY?

	S	M	T	W	TH	F	S
WEEK 1							
WEEK 2							
WEEK 3							
WEEK 4							

IF NOT, WHAT ARE YOU WAITING FOR? GET OUTSIDE AND PLAY!

SLEEP TRACKER

HOW MANY HOURS OF SLEEP DID YOU GET LAST NIGHT?

	S	M	T	W	TH	F	S
Week 1							
Week 2							
Week 3							
Week 4							

IN ORDER TO GET 8 HOURS OF SLEEP, I NEED TO GO TO SLEEP BY ___

THIS WEEK

FAVORITE ACTIVITY

FAVORITE THING I LEARNED

FAVORITE MEAL

LEAST FAVORITE THING

WEEKLY GOALS

WHAT ARE YOU PUTTING EFFORT IN TO GET ACCOMPLISHED THIS WEEK?

_____

_____

_____

_____

WHAT IS YOUR AFFIMATION FOR THE WEEK?

_____

RISING CHECKLIST

Morning Tasks   Mon   Tues   Wed   Thurs   Fri

_____

_____

_____

_____

_____

_____

_____

_____

Checklist SUGGESTIONS

wake up when alarm goes off	brush teeth	eat breakfast	make bed	get dressed
clean up	wash face	shoes/ jacket	put homework in backpack	brush hair
pack a lunch	feed the pet	clean out school folder	take vitamins/ medications	gather important school papers
clear dishes from breakfast	put pajamas in clothes hamper	make snack for school	double-check backpack	grab lunch and devices
use the bathroom	avoid technology	get school notes signed	hugs and kisses	turn off all the lights

WEEKLY CHORE TRACKER

WEEK OF _____

	M	T	W	T	F	S	S

	M	T	W	T	F	S	S

	M	T	W	T	F	S	S

HOMEWORK TRACKER

Week: _____

Assignment	Time Spent	Due date	✓
1. _____	_____	_____	☐
2. _____	_____	_____	☐
3. _____	_____	_____	☐
4. _____	_____	_____	☐
5. _____	_____	_____	☐
6. _____	_____	_____	☐
7. _____	_____	_____	☐
8. _____	_____	_____	☐
9. _____	_____	_____	☐
10. _____	_____	_____	☐
11. _____	_____	_____	☐
12. _____	_____	_____	☐
13. _____	_____	_____	☐
14. _____	_____	_____	☐

Homework Tracker

Week: _____

Assignment	Time Spent	Due date	✓
1. _____	_____	_____	☐
2. _____	_____	_____	☐
3. _____	_____	_____	☐
4. _____	_____	_____	☐
5. _____	_____	_____	☐
6. _____	_____	_____	☐
7. _____	_____	_____	☐
8. _____	_____	_____	☐
9. _____	_____	_____	☐
10. _____	_____	_____	☐
11. _____	_____	_____	☐
12. _____	_____	_____	☐
13. _____	_____	_____	☐
14. _____	_____	_____	☐

EVENING CHECKLIST

Morning Tasks   Mon   Tues   Wed   Thurs   Fri

_____

_____

_____

_____

_____

_____

_____

Checklist SUGGESTIONS

read	listen to music	journal	recite affirmations	set goals
evening drink	take a bath/ shower	unplug	clean up	pack bag
lay out uniform	make lunch	homework	chores	laundry
empty out lunch bag	feed pets	pick out clothes for the next day	charge devices	put on pajamas
brush teeth	go to bathroom	take vitamins/ medications	double-check or set a wake-up alarm	go to sleep early

ACTIVITY TRACKER

WERE YOU ACTIVE TODAY?

	S	M	T	W	TH	F	S
WEEK 1							
WEEK 2							
WEEK 3							
WEEK 4							

IF NOT, WHAT ARE YOU WAITING FOR? GET OUTSIDE AND PLAY!

SLEEP TRACKER

HOW MANY HOURS OF SLEEP DID YOU GET LAST NIGHT?

	S	M	T	W	TH	F	S
Week 1							
Week 2							
Week 3							
Week 4							

IN ORDER TO GET 8 HOURS OF SLEEP, I NEED TO GO TO SLEEP BY

THIS WEEK

FAVORITE ACTIVITY

FAVORITE THING I LEARNED

FAVORITE MEAL

LEAST FAVORITE THING

WEEKLY GOALS

WHAT ARE YOU PUTTING EFFORT IN TO GET ACCOMPLISHED THIS WEEK?

_____
_____
_____
_____

WHAT IS YOUR AFFIMATION FOR THE WEEK?

_____

RISING CHECKLIST

Morning Tasks   Mon   Tues   Wed   Thurs   Fri

_____

_____

_____

_____

_____

_____

_____

Checklist SUGGESTIONS

wake up when alarm goes off	brush teeth	eat breakfast	make bed	get dressed
clean up	wash face	shoes/ jacket	put homework in backpack	brush hair
pack a lunch	feed the pet	clean out school folder	take vitamins/ medications	gather important school papers
clear dishes from breakfast	put pajamas in clothes hamper	make snack for school	double-check backpack	grab lunch and devices
use the bathroom	avoid technology	get school notes signed	hugs and kisses	turn off all the lights

WEEKLY CHORE TRACKER

WEEK OF _____

	M	T	W	T	F	S	S

	M	T	W	T	F	S	S

	M	T	W	T	F	S	S

HOMEWORK TRACKER

Week:

Assignment	Time Spent	Due date	✓
1.			☐
2.			☐
3.			☐
4.			☐
5.			☐
6.			☐
7.			☐
8.			☐
9.			☐
10.			☐
11.			☐
12.			☐
13.			☐
14.			☐

HOMEWORK TRACKER

Week: _____

Assignment	Time Spent	Due date	✓
1. _____	_____	_____	☐
2. _____	_____	_____	☐
3. _____	_____	_____	☐
4. _____	_____	_____	☐
5. _____	_____	_____	☐
6. _____	_____	_____	☐
7. _____	_____	_____	☐
8. _____	_____	_____	☐
9. _____	_____	_____	☐
10. _____	_____	_____	☐
11. _____	_____	_____	☐
12. _____	_____	_____	☐
13. _____	_____	_____	☐
14. _____	_____	_____	☐

EVENING CHECKLIST

Morning Tasks Mon Tues Wed Thurs Fri

_____

_____

_____

_____

_____

_____

_____

Checklist SUGGESTIONS

read	listen to music	journal	recite affirmations	set goals
evening drink	take a bath/ shower	unplug	clean up	pack bag
lay out uniform	make lunch	homework	chores	laundry
empty out lunch bag	feed pets	pick out clothes for the next day	charge devices	put on pajamas
brush teeth	go to bathroom	take vitamins/ medications	double-check or set a wake-up alarm	go to sleep early

ACTIVITY TRACKER

WERE YOU ACTIVE TODAY?

	S	M	T	W	TH	F	S
WEEK 1							
WEEK 2							
WEEK 3							
WEEK 4							

IF NOT, WHAT ARE YOU WAITING FOR? GET OUTSIDE AND PLAY!

SLEEP TRACKER

HOW MANY HOURS OF SLEEP DID YOU GET LAST NIGHT?

	S	M	T	W	TH	F	S
Week 1							
Week 2							
Week 3							
Week 4							

IN ORDER TO GET 8 HOURS OF SLEEP, I NEED TO GO TO SLEEP BY ___

THIS WEEK

FAVORITE ACTIVITY

FAVORITE THING I LEARNED

FAVORITE MEAL

LEAST FAVORITE THING

END OF THE MONTH RECAP

SMALL WINS

1. _____
2. _____
3. _____

BIG ACHIEVEMENTS

1. _____
2. _____
3. _____

HIGHLIGHTS

_____
_____
_____
_____

LESSONS I LEARNED

_____
_____
_____
_____

WHAT WORKED WELL FOR ME

_____
_____
_____
_____
_____
_____

WHAT I'LL STOP DOING

_____
_____
_____
_____
_____
_____

IMPROVEMENTS TO MAKE

_____
_____
_____
_____

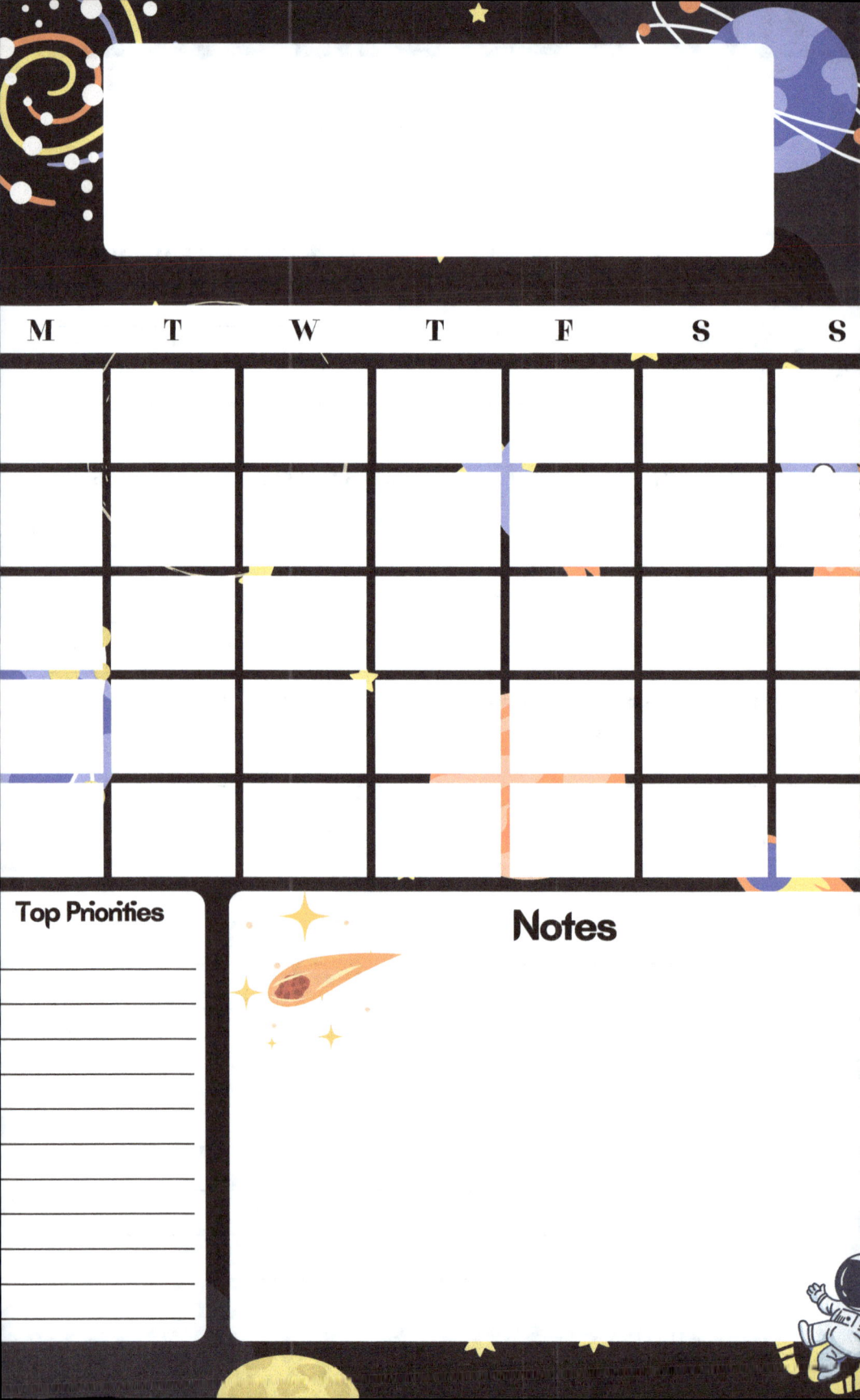

MONTHLY CHORE ASSIGNMENTS

What chores have your parents assigned you? (Grab a parent to help you fill out this page if you are not sure.)

DAILY CHORES

Kitchen
_____
_____
_____

Bathroom
_____
_____
_____

Living Room
_____
_____
_____

Bedroom
_____
_____
_____

WEEKLY CHORES

Kitchen
_____
_____
_____

Bathroom
_____
_____
_____

Living Room
_____
_____
_____

Bedroom
_____
_____
_____

EMOTIONS TRACKER

KEY

EVERY DAY FILL IN A SMALL PIECE OF THE PICTURE WITH THE COLOR LISTED FOR HOW YOU FELT TODAY

 HAPPY  EXCITED  WORRIED

 SAD  MAD  ANGRY

DAILY GRATITUDE LOG

WRITE DOWN 3 THINGS YOU ARE GRATEFUL FOR ON EACH LINE

1. ....
2. ....
3. ....
4. ....
5. ....
6. ....
7. ....
8. ....
9. ....
10. ....
11. ....
12. ....
13. ....
14. ....
15. ....
16. ....
17. ....
18. ....
19. ....
20. ....
21. ....
22. ....
23. ....
24. ....
25. ....
26. ....
27. ....
28. ....
29. ....
30. ....
31. ....

WEEKLY GOALS

WHAT ARE YOU PUTTING EFFORT IN TO GET ACCOMPLISHED THIS WEEK?

_____
_____
_____
_____

WHAT IS YOUR AFFIMATION FOR THE WEEK?

_____

RISING CHECKLIST

Morning Tasks   Mon   Tues   Wed   Thurs   Fri

_____

_____

_____

_____

_____

_____

_____

_____

Checklist SUGGESTIONS

wake up when alarm goes off	brush teeth	eat breakfast	make bed	get dressed
clean up	wash face	shoes/ jacket	put homework in backpack	brush hair
pack a lunch	feed the pet	clean out school folder	take vitamins/ medications	gather important school papers
clear dishes from breakfast	put pajamas in clothes hamper	make snack for school	double-check backpack	grab lunch and devices
use the bathroom	avoid technology	get school notes signed	hugs and kisses	turn off all the lights

WEEKLY CHORE TRACKER

WEEK OF _____

	M	T	W	T	F	S	S

	M	T	W	T	F	S	S

	M	T	W	T	F	S	S

Homework Tracker

Week: _____

Assignment	Time Spent	Due date	✓
1. _____	_____	_____	☐
2. _____	_____	_____	☐
3. _____	_____	_____	☐
4. _____	_____	_____	☐
5. _____	_____	_____	☐
6. _____	_____	_____	☐
7. _____	_____	_____	☐
8. _____	_____	_____	☐
9. _____	_____	_____	☐
10. _____	_____	_____	☐
11. _____	_____	_____	☐
12. _____	_____	_____	☐
13. _____	_____	_____	☐
14. _____	_____	_____	☐

Homework Tracker

Week: _____

Assignment	Time Spent	Due date	✓
1. _____	_____	_____	☐
2. _____	_____	_____	☐
3. _____	_____	_____	☐
4. _____	_____	_____	☐
5. _____	_____	_____	☐
6. _____	_____	_____	☐
7. _____	_____	_____	☐
8. _____	_____	_____	☐
9. _____	_____	_____	☐
10. _____	_____	_____	☐
11. _____	_____	_____	☐
12. _____	_____	_____	☐
13. _____	_____	_____	☐
14. _____	_____	_____	☐

EVENING CHECKLIST

Morning Tasks   Mon   Tues   Wed   Thurs   Fri

_____   ○   ○   ○   ○   ○

_____   ○   ○   ○   ○   ○

_____   ○   ○   ○   ○   ○

_____   ○   ○   ○   ○   ○

_____   ○   ○   ○   ○   ○

_____   ○   ○   ○   ○   ○

_____   ○   ○   ○   ○   ○

_____   ○   ○   ○   ○   ○

Checklist SUGGESTIONS

read	listen to music	journal	recite affirmations	set goals
evening drink	take a bath/ shower	unplug	clean up	pack bag
lay out uniform	make lunch	homework	chores	laundry
empty out lunch bag	feed pets	pick out clothes for the next day	charge devices	put on pajamas
brush teeth	go to bathroom	take vitamins/ medications	double-check or set a wake-up alarm	go to sleep early

ACTIVITY TRACKER

WERE YOU ACTIVE TODAY?

	S	M	T	W	TH	F	S
WEEK 1							
WEEK 2							
WEEK 3							
WEEK 4							

IF NOT, WHAT ARE YOU WAITING FOR? GET OUTSIDE AND PLAY!

SLEEP TRACKER

HOW MANY HOURS OF SLEEP DID YOU GET LAST NIGHT?

	S	M	T	W	TH	F	S
Week 1							
Week 2							
Week 3							
Week 4							

IN ORDER TO GET 8 HOURS OF SLEEP, I NEED TO GO TO SLEEP BY

THIS WEEK

FAVORITE ACTIVITY

FAVORITE THING I LEARNED

FAVORITE MEAL

LEAST FAVORITE THING

WEEKLY GOALS

WHAT ARE YOU PUTTING EFFORT IN TO GET ACCOMPLISHED THIS WEEK?

_____
_____
_____
_____

WHAT IS YOUR AFFIMATION FOR THE WEEK?

_____

RISING CHECKLIST

Morning Tasks   Mon   Tues   Wed   Thurs   Fri

_____

_____

_____

_____

_____

_____

_____

_____

wake up when alarm goes off	brush teeth	eat breakfast	make bed	get dressed
clean up	wash face	shoes/ jacket	put homework in backpack	brush hair
pack a lunch	feed the pet	clean out school folder	take vitamins/ medications	gather important school papers
clear dishes from breakfast	put pajamas in clothes hamper	make snack for school	double-check backpack	grab lunch and devices
use the bathroom	avoid technology	get school notes signed	hugs and kisses	turn off all the lights

Checklist SUGGESTIONS

WEEKLY CHORE TRACKER

WEEK OF _____

	M	T	W	T	F	S	S

	M	T	W	T	F	S	S

	M	T	W	T	F	S	S

HOMEWORK TRACKER

Week: _____

Assignment	Time Spent	Due date	✓
1. _____	_____	_____	☐
2. _____	_____	_____	☐
3. _____	_____	_____	☐
4. _____	_____	_____	☐
5. _____	_____	_____	☐
6. _____	_____	_____	☐
7. _____	_____	_____	☐
8. _____	_____	_____	☐
9. _____	_____	_____	☐
10. _____	_____	_____	☐
11. _____	_____	_____	☐
12. _____	_____	_____	☐
13. _____	_____	_____	☐
14. _____	_____	_____	☐

Homework Tracker

Week: _____

Assignment	Time Spent	Due date	✓
1. _____	_____	_____	☐
2. _____	_____	_____	☐
3. _____	_____	_____	☐
4. _____	_____	_____	☐
5. _____	_____	_____	☐
6. _____	_____	_____	☐
7. _____	_____	_____	☐
8. _____	_____	_____	☐
9. _____	_____	_____	☐
10. _____	_____	_____	☐
11. _____	_____	_____	☐
12. _____	_____	_____	☐
13. _____	_____	_____	☐
14. _____	_____	_____	☐

EVENING CHECKLIST

Morning Tasks	Mon	Tues	Wed	Thurs	Fri
_____	○	○	○	○	○
_____	○	○	○	○	○
_____	○	○	○	○	○
_____	○	○	○	○	○
_____	○	○	○	○	○
_____	○	○	○	○	○
_____	○	○	○	○	○
_____	○	○	○	○	○

Checklist SUGGESTIONS

read	listen to music	journal	recite affirmations	set goals
evening drink	take a bath/shower	unplug	clean up	pack bag
lay out uniform	make lunch	homework	chores	laundry
empty out lunch bag	feed pets	pick out clothes for the next day	charge devices	put on pajamas
brush teeth	go to bathroom	take vitamins/medications	double-check or set a wake-up alarm	go to sleep early

ACTIVITY TRACKER

WERE YOU ACTIVE TODAY?

	S	M	T	W	TH	F	S
WEEK 1							
WEEK 2							
WEEK 3							
WEEK 4							

IF NOT, WHAT ARE YOU WAITING FOR? GET OUTSIDE AND PLAY!

SLEEP TRACKER

HOW MANY HOURS OF SLEEP DID YOU GET LAST NIGHT?

	S	M	T	W	TH	F	S
Week 1							
Week 2							
Week 3							
Week 4							

IN ORDER TO GET 8 HOURS OF SLEEP, I NEED TO GO TO SLEEP BY

THIS WEEK

FAVORITE ACTIVITY

FAVORITE THING I LEARNED

FAVORITE MEAL

LEAST FAVORITE THING

WEEKLY GOALS

WHAT ARE YOU PUTTING EFFORT IN TO GET ACCOMPLISHED THIS WEEK?

_____
_____
_____
_____

WHAT IS YOUR AFFIMATION FOR THE WEEK?

_____

RISING CHECKLIST

Morning Tasks   Mon   Tues   Wed   Thurs   Fri

_____

_____

_____

_____

_____

_____

_____

Checklist SUGGESTIONS

wake up when alarm goes off	brush teeth	eat breakfast	make bed	get dressed
clean up	wash face	shoes/ jacket	put homework in backpack	brush hair
pack a lunch	feed the pet	clean out school folder	take vitamins/ medications	gather important school papers
clear dishes from breakfast	put pajamas in clothes hamper	make snack for school	double-check backpack	grab lunch and devices
use the bathroom	avoid technology	get school notes signed	hugs and kisses	turn off all the lights

WEEKLY CHORE TRACKER

WEEK OF _____

	M	T	W	T	F	S	S

	M	T	W	T	F	S	S

	M	T	W	T	F	S	S

Homework Tracker

Week: _____

Assignment	Time Spent	Due date	✓
1. _____	_____	_____	☐
2. _____	_____	_____	☐
3. _____	_____	_____	☐
4. _____	_____	_____	☐
5. _____	_____	_____	☐
6. _____	_____	_____	☐
7. _____	_____	_____	☐
8. _____	_____	_____	☐
9. _____	_____	_____	☐
10. _____	_____	_____	☐
11. _____	_____	_____	☐
12. _____	_____	_____	☐
13. _____	_____	_____	☐
14. _____	_____	_____	☐

Homework Tracker

Week: _____

Assignment	Time Spent	Due date	✓
1. _____	_____	_____	☐
2. _____	_____	_____	☐
3. _____	_____	_____	☐
4. _____	_____	_____	☐
5. _____	_____	_____	☐
6. _____	_____	_____	☐
7. _____	_____	_____	☐
8. _____	_____	_____	☐
9. _____	_____	_____	☐
10. _____	_____	_____	☐
11. _____	_____	_____	☐
12. _____	_____	_____	☐
13. _____	_____	_____	☐
14. _____	_____	_____	☐

EVENING CHECKLIST

Morning Tasks   Mon   Tues   Wed   Thurs   Fri

_____

_____

_____

_____

_____

_____

_____

Checklist SUGGESTIONS

read	listen to music	journal	recite affirmations	set goals
evening drink	take a bath/ shower	unplug	clean up	pack bag
lay out uniform	make lunch	homework	chores	laundry
empty out lunch bag	feed pets	pick out clothes for the next day	charge devices	put on pajamas
brush teeth	go to bathroom	take vitamins/ medications	double-check or set a wake-up alarm	go to sleep early

ACTIVITY TRACKER

WERE YOU ACTIVE TODAY?

	S	M	T	W	TH	F	S
WEEK 1							
WEEK 2							
WEEK 3							
WEEK 4							

IF NOT, WHAT ARE YOU WAITING FOR? GET OUTSIDE AND PLAY!

SLEEP TRACKER

HOW MANY HOURS OF SLEEP DID YOU GET LAST NIGHT?

	S	M	T	W	TH	F	S
Week 1							
Week 2							
Week 3							
Week 4							

IN ORDER TO GET 8 HOURS OF SLEEP, I NEED TO GO TO SLEEP BY

THIS WEEK

FAVORITE ACTIVITY

FAVORITE THING I LEARNED

FAVORITE MEAL

LEAST FAVORITE THING

WEEKLY GOALS

WHAT ARE YOU PUTTING EFFORT IN TO GET ACCOMPLISHED THIS WEEK?

_____

_____

_____

_____

WHAT IS YOUR AFFIMATION FOR THE WEEK?

_____

RISING CHECKLIST

Morning Tasks   Mon   Tues   Wed   Thurs   Fri

_____

_____

_____

_____

_____

_____

_____

_____

Checklist SUGGESTIONS

wake up when alarm goes off	brush teeth	eat breakfast	make bed	get dressed
clean up	wash face	shoes/ jacket	put homework in backpack	brush hair
pack a lunch	feed the pet	clean out school folder	take vitamins/ medications	gather important school papers
clear dishes from breakfast	put pajamas in clothes hamper	make snack for school	double- check backpack	grab lunch and devices
use the bathroom	avoid technology	get school notes signed	hugs and kisses	turn off all the lights

WEEKLY CHORE TRACKER

WEEK OF _____

	M	T	W	T	F	S	S

	M	T	W	T	F	S	S

	M	T	W	T	F	S	S

Homework Tracker

Week: _____

Assignment	Time Spent	Due date	✓
1. _____	_____	_____	☐
2. _____	_____	_____	☐
3. _____	_____	_____	☐
4. _____	_____	_____	☐
5. _____	_____	_____	☐
6. _____	_____	_____	☐
7. _____	_____	_____	☐
8. _____	_____	_____	☐
9. _____	_____	_____	☐
10. _____	_____	_____	☐
11. _____	_____	_____	☐
12. _____	_____	_____	☐
13. _____	_____	_____	☐
14. _____	_____	_____	☐

HOMEWORK TRACKER

Week: _____

Assignment	Time Spent	Due date	✓
1. _____	_____	_____	☐
2. _____	_____	_____	☐
3. _____	_____	_____	☐
4. _____	_____	_____	☐
5. _____	_____	_____	☐
6. _____	_____	_____	☐
7. _____	_____	_____	☐
8. _____	_____	_____	☐
9. _____	_____	_____	☐
10. _____	_____	_____	☐
11. _____	_____	_____	☐
12. _____	_____	_____	☐
13. _____	_____	_____	☐
14. _____	_____	_____	☐

EVENING CHECKLIST

Morning Tasks

	Mon	Tues	Wed	Thurs	Fri
_____	○	○	○	○	○
_____	○	○	○	○	○
_____	○	○	○	○	○
_____	○	○	○	○	○
_____	○	○	○	○	○
_____	○	○	○	○	○
_____	○	○	○	○	○
_____	○	○	○	○	○

Checklist SUGGESTIONS

read	listen to music	journal	recite affirmations	set goals
evening drink	take a bath/ shower	unplug	clean up	pack bag
lay out uniform	make lunch	homework	chores	laundry
empty out lunch bag	feed pets	pick out clothes for the next day	charge devices	put on pajamas
brush teeth	go to bathroom	take vitamins/ medications	double-check or set a wake-up alarm	go to sleep early

ACTIVITY TRACKER

WERE YOU ACTIVE TODAY?

	S	M	T	W	TH	F	S
WEEK 1							
WEEK 2							
WEEK 3							
WEEK 4							

IF NOT, WHAT ARE YOU WAITING FOR? GET OUTSIDE AND PLAY!

SLEEP TRACKER

HOW MANY HOURS OF SLEEP DID YOU GET LAST NIGHT?

	S	M	T	W	TH	F	S
Week 1							
Week 2							
Week 3							
Week 4							

IN ORDER TO GET 8 HOURS OF SLEEP, I NEED TO GO TO SLEEP BY

THIS WEEK

FAVORITE ACTIVITY

FAVORITE THING I LEARNED

FAVORITE MEAL

LEAST FAVORITE THING

END OF THE MONTH RECAP

SMALL WINS

1. _____
2. _____
3. _____

BIG ACHIEVEMENTS

1. _____
2. _____
3. _____

HIGHLIGHTS

_____
_____
_____
_____

LESSONS I LEARNED

_____
_____
_____
_____

WHAT WORKED WELL FOR ME

_____
_____
_____
_____
_____
_____

WHAT I'LL STOP DOING

_____
_____
_____
_____
_____
_____

IMPROVEMENTS TO MAKE

_____
_____
_____
_____

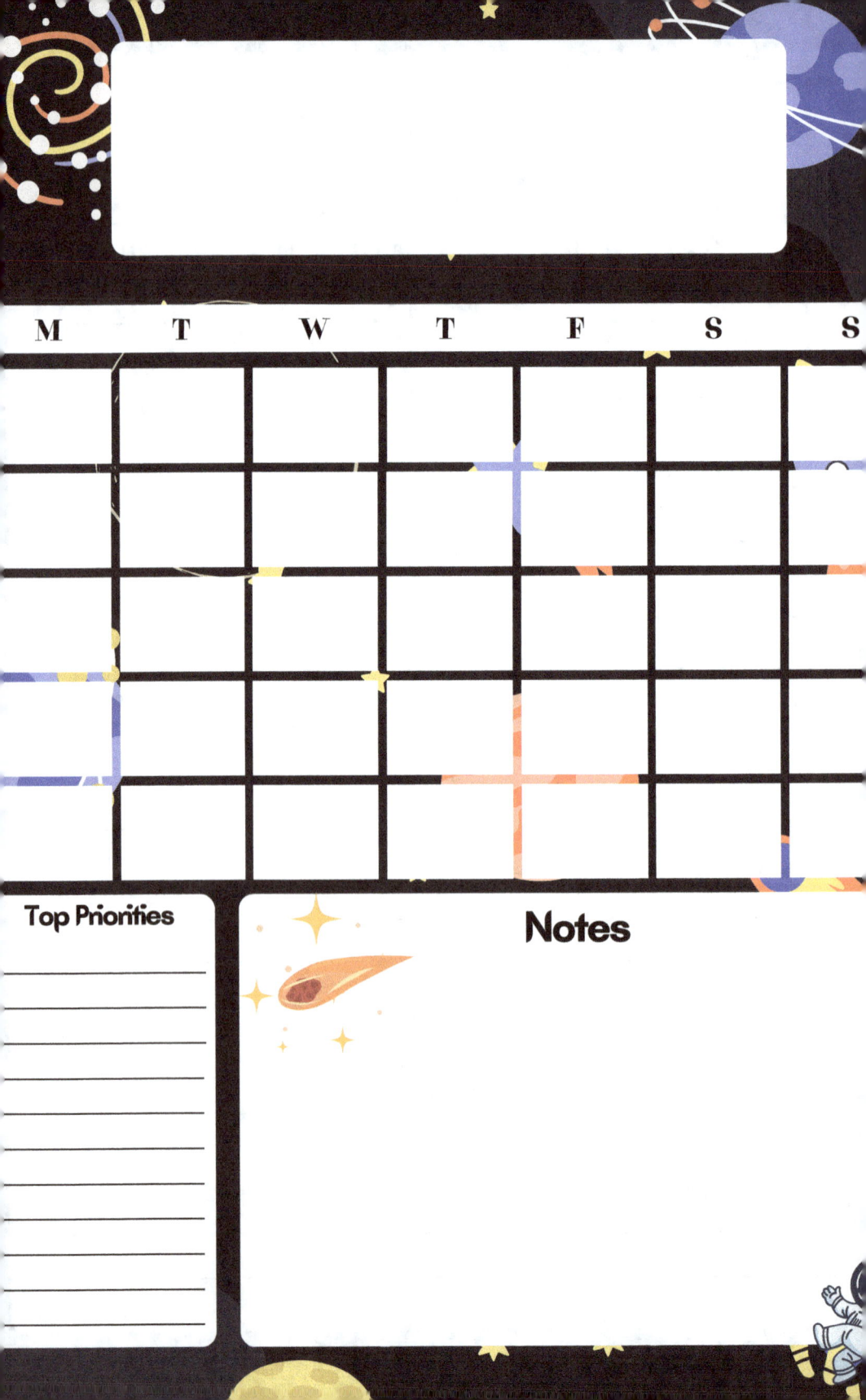

MONTHLY CHORE ASSIGNMENTS

What chores have your parents assigned you? (Grab a parent to help you fill out this page if you are not sure.)

DAILY CHORES

Kitchen
_____
_____
_____

Bathroom
_____
_____
_____

Living Room
_____
_____
_____

Bedroom
_____
_____

WEEKLY CHORES

Kitchen
_____
_____
_____

Bathroom
_____
_____
_____

Living Room
_____
_____
_____

Bedroom
_____
_____

EMOTIONS TRACKER

KEY — EVERY DAY FILL IN A SMALL PIECE OF THE PICTURE WITH THE COLOR LISTED FOR HOW YOU FELT TODAY

 HAPPY    EXCITED    WORRIED

 SAD    MAD    ANGRY

DAILY GRATITUDE LOG

WRITE DOWN 3 THINGS YOU ARE GRATEFUL FOR ON EACH LINE

1. ....
2. ....
3. ....
4. ....
5. ....
6. ....
7. ....
8. ....
9. ....
10. ....
11. ....
12. ....
13. ....
14. ....
15. ....
16. ....
17. ....
18. ....
19. ....
20. ....
21. ....
22. ....
23. ....
24. ....
25. ....
26. ....
27. ....
28. ....
29. ....
30. ....
31. ....

WEEKLY
GOALS

WHAT ARE YOU PUTTING EFFORT IN TO GET ACCOMPLISHED THIS WEEK?

_____

_____

_____

_____

WHAT IS YOUR AFFIMATION FOR THE WEEK?

_____

RISING CHECKLIST

Morning Tasks	Mon	Tues	Wed	Thurs	Fri
_____	○	○	○	○	○
_____	○	○	○	○	○
_____	○	○	○	○	○
_____	○	○	○	○	○
_____	○	○	○	○	○
_____	○	○	○	○	○
_____	○	○	○	○	○
_____	○	○	○	○	○

Checklist SUGGESTIONS

wake up when alarm goes off	brush teeth	eat breakfast	make bed	get dressed
clean up	wash face	shoes/ jacket	put homework in backpack	brush hair
pack a lunch	feed the pet	clean out school folder	take vitamins/ medications	gather important school papers
clear dishes from breakfast	put pajamas in clothes hamper	make snack for school	double-check backpack	grab lunch and devices
use the bathroom	avoid technology	get school notes signed	hugs and kisses	turn off all the lights

WEEKLY CHORE TRACKER

WEEK OF _____

	M	T	W	T	F	S	S

	M	T	W	T	F	S	S

	M	T	W	T	F	S	S

HOMEWORK TRACKER

Week: _____

Assignment	Time Spent	Due date	✓
1. _____	_____	_____	☐
2. _____	_____	_____	☐
3. _____	_____	_____	☐
4. _____	_____	_____	☐
5. _____	_____	_____	☐
6. _____	_____	_____	☐
7. _____	_____	_____	☐
8. _____	_____	_____	☐
9. _____	_____	_____	☐
10. _____	_____	_____	☐
11. _____	_____	_____	☐
12. _____	_____	_____	☐
13. _____	_____	_____	☐
14. _____	_____	_____	☐

HOMEWORK TRACKER

Week: _____

Assignment	Time Spent	Due date	✓
1. _____	_____	_____	☐
2. _____	_____	_____	☐
3. _____	_____	_____	☐
4. _____	_____	_____	☐
5. _____	_____	_____	☐
6. _____	_____	_____	☐
7. _____	_____	_____	☐
8. _____	_____	_____	☐
9. _____	_____	_____	☐
10. _____	_____	_____	☐
11. _____	_____	_____	☐
12. _____	_____	_____	☐
13. _____	_____	_____	☐
14. _____	_____	_____	☐

EVENING CHECKLIST

Morning Tasks   Mon   Tues   Wed   Thurs   Fri

_____

_____

_____

_____

_____

_____

_____

Checklist SUGGESTIONS

read	listen to music	journal	recite affirmations	set goals
evening drink	take a bath/ shower	unplug	clean up	pack bag
lay out uniform	make lunch	homework	chores	laundry
empty out lunch bag	feed pets	pick out clothes for the next day	charge devices	put on pajamas
brush teeth	go to bathroom	take vitamins/ medications	double-check or set a wake-up alarm	go to sleep early

ACTIVITY TRACKER

WERE YOU ACTIVE TODAY?

	S	M	T	W	TH	F	S
WEEK 1							
WEEK 2							
WEEK 3							
WEEK 4							

IF NOT, WHAT ARE YOU WAITING FOR? GET OUTSIDE AND PLAY!

SLEEP TRACKER

HOW MANY HOURS OF SLEEP DID YOU GET LAST NIGHT?

	S	M	T	W	TH	F	S
Week 1							
Week 2							
Week 3							
Week 4							

IN ORDER TO GET 8 HOURS OF SLEEP, I NEED TO GO TO SLEEP BY

THIS WEEK

FAVORITE ACTIVITY

FAVORITE THING I LEARNED

FAVORITE MEAL

LEAST FAVORITE THING

WEEKLY
GOALS

WHAT ARE YOU PUTTING EFFORT IN TO GET ACCOMPLISHED THIS WEEK?

_____
_____
_____
_____

WHAT IS YOUR AFFIMATION FOR THE WEEK?

_____

RISING CHECKLIST

Morning Tasks Mon Tues Wed Thurs Fri

_____

_____

_____

_____

_____

_____

_____

_____

Checklist SUGGESTIONS

wake up when alarm goes off	brush teeth	eat breakfast	make bed	get dressed
clean up	wash face	shoes/ jacket	put homework in backpack	brush hair
pack a lunch	feed the pet	clean out school folder	take vitamins/ medications	gather important school papers
clear dishes from breakfast	put pajamas in clothes hamper	make snack for school	double-check backpack	grab lunch and devices
use the bathroom	avoid technology	get school notes signed	hugs and kisses	turn off all the lights

WEEKLY CHORE TRACKER

WEEK OF _____

	M	T	W	T	F	S	S

	M	T	W	T	F	S	S

	M	T	W	T	F	S	S

HOMEWORK TRACKER

Week: _____

Assignment	Time Spent	Due date	✓
1. _____	_____	_____	☐
2. _____	_____	_____	☐
3. _____	_____	_____	☐
4. _____	_____	_____	☐
5. _____	_____	_____	☐
6. _____	_____	_____	☐
7. _____	_____	_____	☐
8. _____	_____	_____	☐
9. _____	_____	_____	☐
10. _____	_____	_____	☐
11. _____	_____	_____	☐
12. _____	_____	_____	☐
13. _____	_____	_____	☐
14. _____	_____	_____	☐

Homework Tracker

Week:

Assignment	Time Spent	Due date	✓
1. _____	_____	_____	☐
2. _____	_____	_____	☐
3. _____	_____	_____	☐
4. _____	_____	_____	☐
5. _____	_____	_____	☐
6. _____	_____	_____	☐
7. _____	_____	_____	☐
8. _____	_____	_____	☐
9. _____	_____	_____	☐
10. _____	_____	_____	☐
11. _____	_____	_____	☐
12. _____	_____	_____	☐
13. _____	_____	_____	☐
14. _____	_____	_____	☐

EVENING CHECKLIST

Morning Tasks   Mon   Tues   Wed   Thurs   Fri

_____

_____

_____

_____

_____

_____

_____

_____

read	listen to music	journal	recite affirmations	set goals	
evening drink	take a bath/ shower	unplug	clean up	pack bag	Checklist SUGGESTIONS
lay out uniform	make lunch	homework	chores	laundry	
empty out lunch bag	feed pets	pick out clothes for the next day	charge devices	put on pajamas	
brush teeth	go to bathroom	take vitamins/ medications	double-check or set a wake-up alarm	go to sleep early	

ACTIVITY TRACKER

WERE YOU ACTIVE TODAY?

	S	M	T	W	TH	F	S
WEEK 1							
WEEK 2							
WEEK 3							
WEEK 4							

IF NOT, WHAT ARE YOU WAITING FOR? GET OUTSIDE AND PLAY!

SLEEP TRACKER

HOW MANY HOURS OF SLEEP DID YOU GET LAST NIGHT?

	S	M	T	W	TH	F	S
Week 1							
Week 2							
Week 3							
Week 4							

IN ORDER TO GET 8 HOURS OF SLEEP, I NEED TO GO TO SLEEP BY

THIS WEEK

FAVORITE ACTIVITY

FAVORITE THING I LEARNED

FAVORITE MEAL

LEAST FAVORITE THING

WEEKLY GOALS

WHAT ARE YOU PUTTING EFFORT IN TO GET ACCOMPLISHED THIS WEEK?

_____
_____
_____
_____

WHAT IS YOUR AFFIMATION FOR THE WEEK?

_____

RISING CHECKLIST

Morning Tasks   Mon   Tues   Wed   Thurs   Fri

_____

_____

_____

_____

_____

_____

_____

Checklist SUGGESTIONS

wake up when alarm goes off	brush teeth	eat breakfast	make bed	get dressed
clean up	wash face	shoes/ jacket	put homework in backpack	brush hair
pack a lunch	feed the pet	clean out school folder	take vitamins/ medications	gather important school papers
clear dishes from breakfast	put pajamas in clothes hamper	make snack for school	double-check backpack	grab lunch and devices
use the bathroom	avoid technology	get school notes signed	hugs and kisses	turn off all the lights

WEEKLY CHORE TRACKER

WEEK OF _____

	M	T	W	T	F	S	S

	M	T	W	T	F	S	S

	M	T	W	T	F	S	S

HOMEWORK TRACKER

Week: _____

Assignment	Time Spent	Due date	✓
1. _____	_____	_____	☐
2. _____	_____	_____	☐
3. _____	_____	_____	☐
4. _____	_____	_____	☐
5. _____	_____	_____	☐
6. _____	_____	_____	☐
7. _____	_____	_____	☐
8. _____	_____	_____	☐
9. _____	_____	_____	☐
10. _____	_____	_____	☐
11. _____	_____	_____	☐
12. _____	_____	_____	☐
13. _____	_____	_____	☐
14. _____	_____	_____	☐

Homework Tracker

Week: _____

Assignment	Time Spent	Due date	✓
1. _____	_____	_____	☐
2. _____	_____	_____	☐
3. _____	_____	_____	☐
4. _____	_____	_____	☐
5. _____	_____	_____	☐
6. _____	_____	_____	☐
7. _____	_____	_____	☐
8. _____	_____	_____	☐
9. _____	_____	_____	☐
10. _____	_____	_____	☐
11. _____	_____	_____	☐
12. _____	_____	_____	☐
13. _____	_____	_____	☐
14. _____	_____	_____	☐

EVENING CHECKLIST

Morning Tasks   Mon   Tues   Wed   Thurs   Fri

_____

_____

_____

_____

_____

_____

_____

Checklist SUGGESTIONS

read	listen to music	journal	recite affirmations	set goals
evening drink	take a bath/ shower	unplug	clean up	pack bag
lay out uniform	make lunch	homework	chores	laundry
empty out lunch bag	feed pets	pick out clothes for the next day	charge devices	put on pajamas
brush teeth	go to bathroom	take vitamins/ medications	double-check or set a wake-up alarm	go to sleep early

ACTIVITY TRACKER

WERE YOU ACTIVE TODAY?

	S	M	T	W	TH	F	S
WEEK 1							
WEEK 2							
WEEK 3							
WEEK 4							

IF NOT, WHAT ARE YOU WAITING FOR? GET OUTSIDE AND PLAY!

SLEEP TRACKER

HOW MANY HOURS OF SLEEP DID YOU GET LAST NIGHT?

	S	M	T	W	TH	F	S
Week 1							
Week 2							
Week 3							
Week 4							

IN ORDER TO GET 8 HOURS OF SLEEP, I NEED TO GO TO SLEEP BY ☐

THIS WEEK

FAVORITE ACTIVITY

FAVORITE THING I LEARNED

FAVORITE MEAL

LEAST FAVORITE THING

WEEKLY
GOALS

WHAT ARE YOU PUTTING EFFORT IN TO GET ACCOMPLISHED THIS WEEK?

_____

_____

_____

_____

WHAT IS YOUR AFFIMATION FOR THE WEEK?

_____

RISING CHECKLIST

Morning Tasks   Mon   Tues   Wed   Thurs   Fri

_____

_____

_____

_____

_____

_____

_____

_____

Checklist SUGGESTIONS

wake up when alarm goes off	brush teeth	eat breakfast	make bed	get dressed
clean up	wash face	shoes/ jacket	put homework in backpack	brush hair
pack a lunch	feed the pet	clean out school folder	take vitamins/ medications	gather important school papers
clear dishes from breakfast	put pajamas in clothes hamper	make snack for school	double-check backpack	grab lunch and devices
use the bathroom	avoid technology	get school notes signed	hugs and kisses	turn off all the lights

WEEKLY CHORE TRACKER

WEEK OF _____

	M	T	W	T	F	S	S

	M	T	W	T	F	S	S

	M	T	W	T	F	S	S

Homework Tracker

Week:

Assignment	Time Spent	Due date	✓
1. _____	_____	_____	☐
2. _____	_____	_____	☐
3. _____	_____	_____	☐
4. _____	_____	_____	☐
5. _____	_____	_____	☐
6. _____	_____	_____	☐
7. _____	_____	_____	☐
8. _____	_____	_____	☐
9. _____	_____	_____	☐
10. _____	_____	_____	☐
11. _____	_____	_____	☐
12. _____	_____	_____	☐
13. _____	_____	_____	☐
14. _____	_____	_____	☐

Homework Tracker

Week: _____

Assignment	Time Spent	Due date	✓
1. _____	_____	_____	☐
2. _____	_____	_____	☐
3. _____	_____	_____	☐
4. _____	_____	_____	☐
5. _____	_____	_____	☐
6. _____	_____	_____	☐
7. _____	_____	_____	☐
8. _____	_____	_____	☐
9. _____	_____	_____	☐
10. _____	_____	_____	☐
11. _____	_____	_____	☐
12. _____	_____	_____	☐
13. _____	_____	_____	☐
14. _____	_____	_____	☐

EVENING CHECKLIST

Morning Tasks   Mon   Tues   Wed   Thurs   Fri

_____

_____

_____

_____

_____

_____

_____

Checklist SUGGESTIONS

read	listen to music	journal	recite affirmations	set goals
evening drink	take a bath/ shower	unplug	clean up	pack bag
lay out uniform	make lunch	homework	chores	laundry
empty out lunch bag	feed pets	pick out clothes for the next day	charge devices	put on pajamas
brush teeth	go to bathroom	take vitamins/ medications	double-check or set a wake-up alarm	go to sleep early

ACTIVITY TRACKER

WERE YOU ACTIVE TODAY?

	S	M	T	W	TH	F	S
WEEK 1							
WEEK 2							
WEEK 3							
WEEK 4							

IF NOT, WHAT ARE YOU WAITING FOR? GET OUTSIDE AND PLAY!

SLEEP TRACKER

HOW MANY HOURS OF SLEEP DID YOU GET LAST NIGHT?

	S	M	T	W	TH	F	S
Week 1							
Week 2							
Week 3							
Week 4							

IN ORDER TO GET 8 HOURS OF SLEEP, I NEED TO GO TO SLEEP BY

THIS WEEK

FAVORITE ACTIVITY

FAVORITE THING I LEARNED

FAVORITE MEAL

LEAST FAVORITE THING

END OF THE MONTH RECAP

SMALL WINS

1. _____
2. _____
3. _____

BIG ACHIEVEMENTS

1. _____
2. _____
3. _____

HIGHLIGHTS

_____
_____
_____
_____

LESSONS I LEARNED

_____
_____
_____
_____

WHAT WORKED WELL FOR ME

_____
_____
_____
_____
_____
_____
_____

WHAT I'LL STOP DOING

_____
_____
_____
_____
_____
_____
_____

IMPROVEMENTS TO MAKE

_____
_____
_____
_____

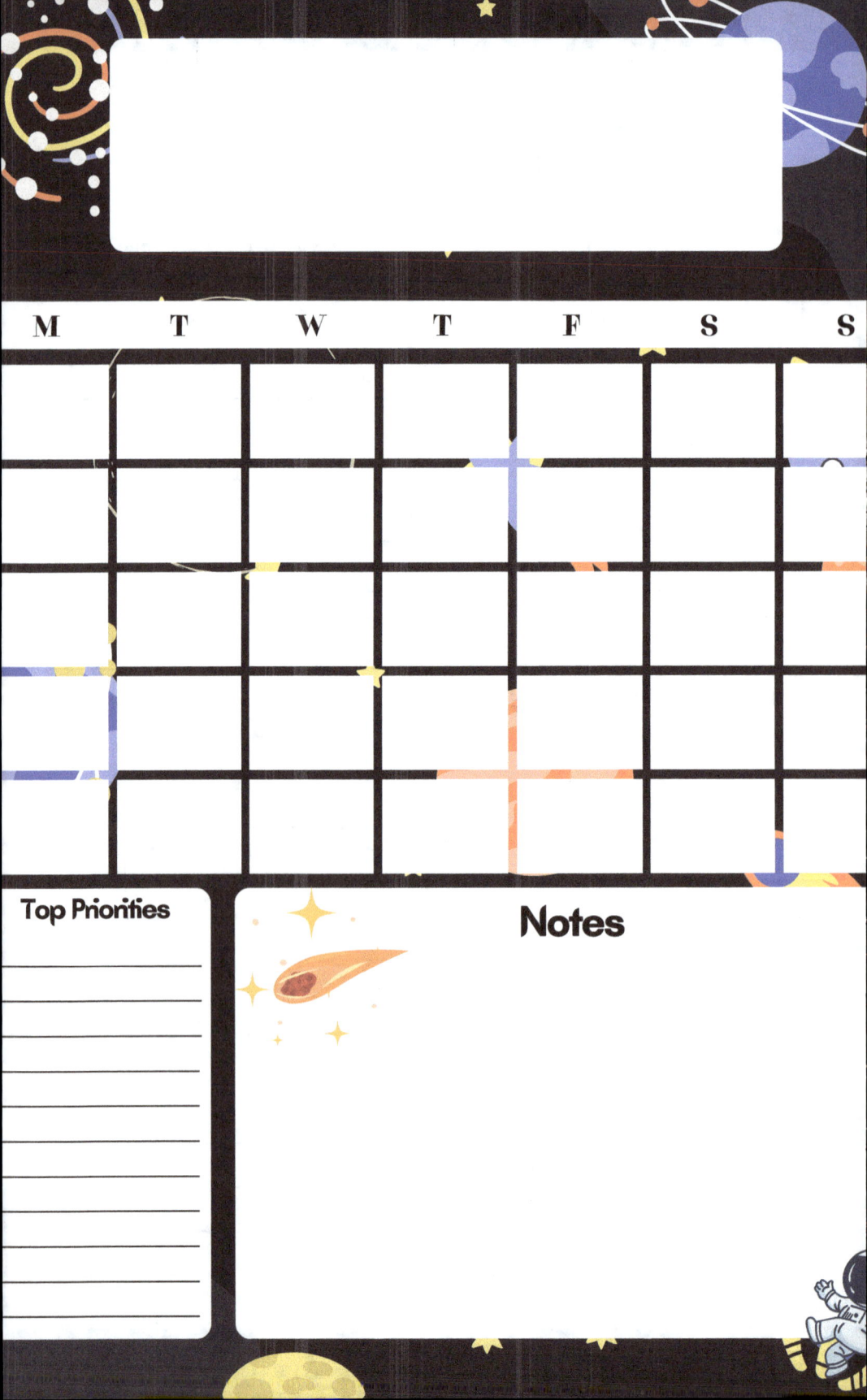

MONTHLY CHORE ASSIGNMENTS

What chores have your parents assigned you? (Grab a parent to help you fill out this page if you are not sure.)

DAILY CHORES

Kitchen
_____
_____
_____

Bathroom
_____
_____
_____

Living Room
_____
_____
_____

Bedroom
_____
_____
_____

WEEKLY CHORES

Kitchen
_____
_____
_____

Bathroom
_____
_____
_____

Living Room
_____
_____
_____

Bedroom
_____
_____
_____

EMOTIONS TRACKER

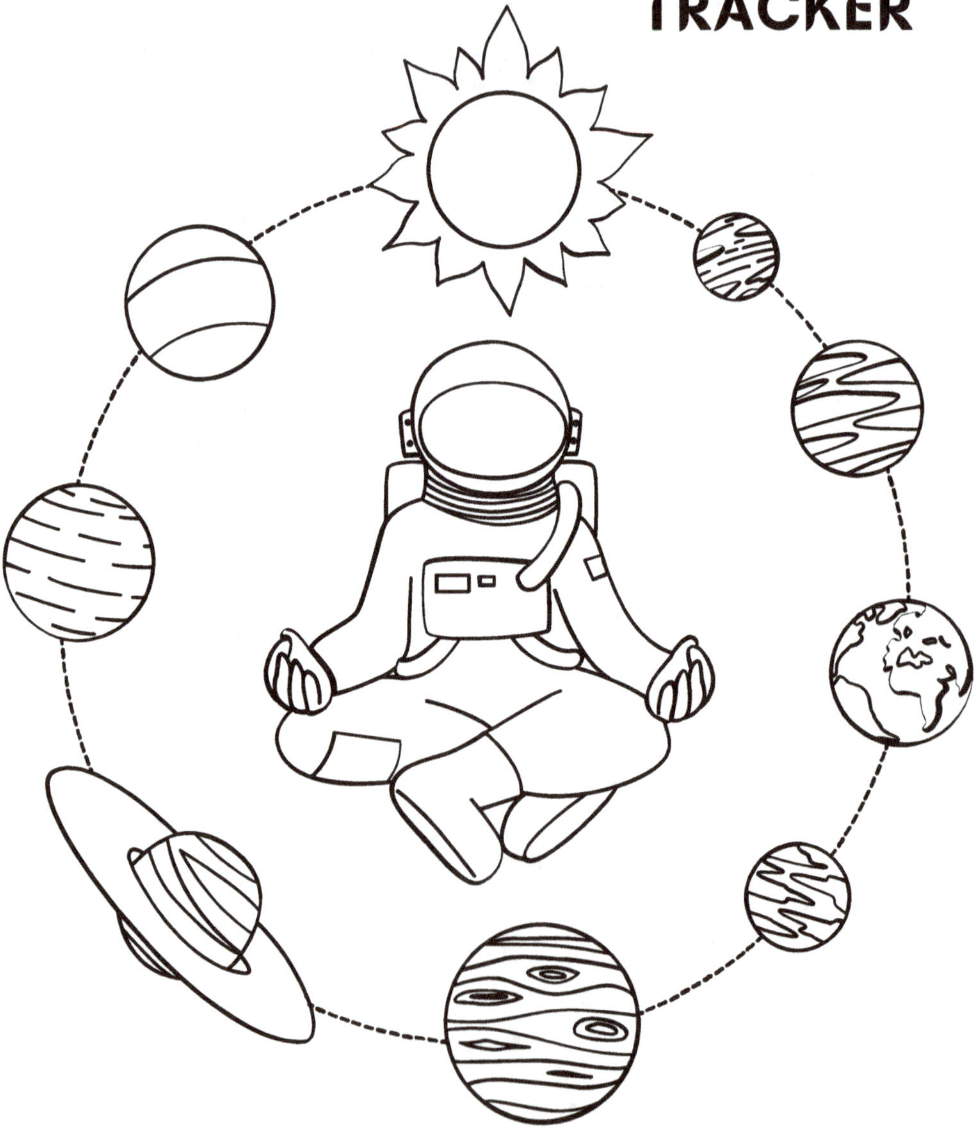

EVERY DAY FILL IN A SMALL PIECE OF THE PICTURE WITH THE COLOR LISTED FOR HOW YOU FELT TODAY

 HAPPY    EXCITED    WORRIED

 SAD    MAD    ANGRY

DAILY GRATITUDE LOG

WRITE DOWN 3 THINGS YOU ARE GRATEFUL FOR ON EACH LINE

1. ....
2. ....
3. ....
4. ....
5. ....
6. ....
7. ....
8. ....
9. ....
10. ....
11. ....
12. ....
13. ....
14. ....
15. ....
16. ....
17. ....
18. ....
19. ....
20. ....
21. ....
22. ....
23. ....
24. ....
25. ....
26. ....
27. ....
28. ....
29. ....
30. ....
31. ....

WEEKLY GOALS

WHAT ARE YOU PUTTING EFFORT IN TO GET ACCOMPLISHED THIS WEEK?

_____

_____

_____

_____

WHAT IS YOUR AFFIMATION FOR THE WEEK?

_____

RISING CHECKLIST

Morning Tasks	Mon	Tues	Wed	Thurs	Fri
_____	○	○	○	○	○
_____	○	○	○	○	○
_____	○	○	○	○	○
_____	○	○	○	○	○
_____	○	○	○	○	○
_____	○	○	○	○	○
_____	○	○	○	○	○
_____	○	○	○	○	○

Checklist SUGGESTIONS

wake up when alarm goes off	brush teeth	eat breakfast	make bed	get dressed
clean up	wash face	shoes/jacket	put homework in backpack	brush hair
pack a lunch	feed the pet	clean out school folder	take vitamins/medications	gather important school papers
clear dishes from breakfast	put pajamas in clothes hamper	make snack for school	double-check backpack	grab lunch and devices
use the bathroom	avoid technology	get school notes signed	hugs and kisses	turn off all the lights

WEEKLY CHORE TRACKER

WEEK OF _____

	M	T	W	T	F	S	S

	M	T	W	T	F	S	S

	M	T	W	T	F	S	S

HOMEWORK TRACKER

Week: _____

Assignment	Time Spent	Due date	✓
1. _____	_____	_____	☐
2. _____	_____	_____	☐
3. _____	_____	_____	☐
4. _____	_____	_____	☐
5. _____	_____	_____	☐
6. _____	_____	_____	☐
7. _____	_____	_____	☐
8. _____	_____	_____	☐
9. _____	_____	_____	☐
10. _____	_____	_____	☐
11. _____	_____	_____	☐
12. _____	_____	_____	☐
13. _____	_____	_____	☐
14. _____	_____	_____	☐

HOMEWORK TRACKER

Week: _____

Assignment	Time Spent	Due date	✓
1. _____	_____	_____	☐
2. _____	_____	_____	☐
3. _____	_____	_____	☐
4. _____	_____	_____	☐
5. _____	_____	_____	☐
6. _____	_____	_____	☐
7. _____	_____	_____	☐
8. _____	_____	_____	☐
9. _____	_____	_____	☐
10. _____	_____	_____	☐
11. _____	_____	_____	☐
12. _____	_____	_____	☐
13. _____	_____	_____	☐
14. _____	_____	_____	☐

EVENING CHECKLIST

Morning Tasks

	Mon	Tues	Wed	Thurs	Fri
	○	○	○	○	○
	○	○	○	○	○
	○	○	○	○	○
	○	○	○	○	○
	○	○	○	○	○
	○	○	○	○	○
	○	○	○	○	○
	○	○	○	○	○

Checklist SUGGESTIONS

read	listen to music	journal	recite affirmations	set goals
evening drink	take a bath/ shower	unplug	clean up	pack bag
lay out uniform	make lunch	homework	chores	laundry
empty out lunch bag	feed pets	pick out clothes for the next day	charge devices	put on pajamas
brush teeth	go to bathroom	take vitamins/ medications	double-check or set a wake-up alarm	go to sleep early

ACTIVITY TRACKER

WERE YOU ACTIVE TODAY?

	S	M	T	W	TH	F	S
WEEK 1							
WEEK 2							
WEEK 3							
WEEK 4							

IF NOT, WHAT ARE YOU WAITING FOR? GET OUTSIDE AND PLAY!

SLEEP TRACKER

HOW MANY HOURS OF SLEEP DID YOU GET LAST NIGHT?

	S	M	T	W	TH	F	S
Week 1							
Week 2							
Week 3							
Week 4							

IN ORDER TO GET 8 HOURS OF SLEEP, I NEED TO GO TO SLEEP BY

THIS WEEK

FAVORITE ACTIVITY

FAVORITE THING I LEARNED

FAVORITE MEAL

LEAST FAVORITE THING

WEEKLY GOALS

WHAT ARE YOU PUTTING EFFORT IN TO GET ACCOMPLISHED THIS WEEK?

_____
_____
_____
_____

WHAT IS YOUR AFFIMATION FOR THE WEEK?

_____

RISING CHECKLIST

Morning Tasks   Mon   Tues   Wed   Thurs   Fri

_____ ○ ○ ○ ○ ○

_____ ○ ○ ○ ○ ○

_____ ○ ○ ○ ○ ○

_____ ○ ○ ○ ○ ○

_____ ○ ○ ○ ○ ○

_____ ○ ○ ○ ○ ○

_____ ○ ○ ○ ○ ○

_____ ○ ○ ○ ○ ○

Checklist SUGGESTIONS

wake up when alarm goes off	brush teeth	eat breakfast	make bed	get dressed
clean up	wash face	shoes/ jacket	put homework in backpack	brush hair
pack a lunch	feed the pet	clean out school folder	take vitamins/ medications	gather important school papers
clear dishes from breakfast	put pajamas in clothes hamper	make snack for school	double-check backpack	grab lunch and devices
use the bathroom	avoid technology	get school notes signed	hugs and kisses	turn off all the lights

WEEKLY CHORE TRACKER

WEEK OF _____

	M	T	W	T	F	S	S

	M	T	W	T	F	S	S

	M	T	W	T	F	S	S

HOMEWORK TRACKER

Week: _____

Assignment	Time Spent	Due date	✓
1. _____	_____	_____	☐
2. _____	_____	_____	☐
3. _____	_____	_____	☐
4. _____	_____	_____	☐
5. _____	_____	_____	☐
6. _____	_____	_____	☐
7. _____	_____	_____	☐
8. _____	_____	_____	☐
9. _____	_____	_____	☐
10. _____	_____	_____	☐
11. _____	_____	_____	☐
12. _____	_____	_____	☐
13. _____	_____	_____	☐
14. _____	_____	_____	☐

Homework Tracker

Week: _____

Assignment	Time Spent	Due date	☑
1. _____	_____	_____	☐
2. _____	_____	_____	☐
3. _____	_____	_____	☐
4. _____	_____	_____	☐
5. _____	_____	_____	☐
6. _____	_____	_____	☐
7. _____	_____	_____	☐
8. _____	_____	_____	☐
9. _____	_____	_____	☐
10. _____	_____	_____	☐
11. _____	_____	_____	☐
12. _____	_____	_____	☐
13. _____	_____	_____	☐
14. _____	_____	_____	☐

EVENING CHECKLIST

Morning Tasks

	Mon	Tues	Wed	Thurs	Fri
_____	○	○	○	○	○
_____	○	○	○	○	○
_____	○	○	○	○	○
_____	○	○	○	○	○
_____	○	○	○	○	○
_____	○	○	○	○	○
_____	○	○	○	○	○
_____	○	○	○	○	○

Checklist SUGGESTIONS

read	listen to music	journal	recite affirmations	set goals
evening drink	take a bath/ shower	unplug	clean up	pack bag
lay out uniform	make lunch	homework	chores	laundry
empty out lunch bag	feed pets	pick out clothes for the next day	charge devices	put on pajamas
brush teeth	go to bathroom	take vitamins/ medications	double-check or set a wake-up alarm	go to sleep early

ACTIVITY TRACKER

WERE YOU ACTIVE TODAY?

	S	M	T	W	TH	F	S
WEEK 1							
WEEK 2							
WEEK 3							
WEEK 4							

IF NOT, WHAT ARE YOU WAITING FOR? GET OUTSIDE AND PLAY!

SLEEP TRACKER

HOW MANY HOURS OF SLEEP DID YOU GET LAST NIGHT?

	S	M	T	W	TH	F	S
Week 1							
Week 2							
Week 3							
Week 4							

IN ORDER TO GET 8 HOURS OF SLEEP, I NEED TO GO TO SLEEP BY

FAVORITE ACTIVITY

FAVORITE THING I LEARNED

FAVORITE MEAL

LEAST FAVORITE THING

WEEKLY GOALS

WHAT ARE YOU PUTTING EFFORT IN TO GET ACCOMPLISHED THIS WEEK?

_____

_____

_____

_____

WHAT IS YOUR AFFIMATION FOR THE WEEK?

_____

RISING CHECKLIST

Morning Tasks   Mon   Tues   Wed   Thurs   Fri

_____

_____

_____

_____

_____

_____

_____

_____

Checklist SUGGESTIONS

wake up when alarm goes off	brush teeth	eat breakfast	make bed	get dressed
clean up	wash face	shoes/ jacket	put homework in backpack	brush hair
pack a lunch	feed the pet	clean out school folder	take vitamins/ medications	gather important school papers
clear dishes from breakfast	put pajamas in clothes hamper	make snack for school	double-check backpack	grab lunch and devices
use the bathroom	avoid technology	get school notes signed	hugs and kisses	turn off all the lights

WEEKLY CHORE TRACKER

WEEK OF _____

	M	T	W	T	F	S	S

	M	T	W	T	F	S	S

	M	T	W	T	F	S	S

Homework Tracker

Week:

Assignment	Time Spent	Due date	✓
1. _____	_____	_____	☐
2. _____	_____	_____	☐
3. _____	_____	_____	☐
4. _____	_____	_____	☐
5. _____	_____	_____	☐
6. _____	_____	_____	☐
7. _____	_____	_____	☐
8. _____	_____	_____	☐
9. _____	_____	_____	☐
10. _____	_____	_____	☐
11. _____	_____	_____	☐
12. _____	_____	_____	☐
13. _____	_____	_____	☐
14. _____	_____	_____	☐

HOMEWORK TRACKER

Week: _____

Assignment	Time Spent	Due date	✓
1. _____	_____	_____	☐
2. _____	_____	_____	☐
3. _____	_____	_____	☐
4. _____	_____	_____	☐
5. _____	_____	_____	☐
6. _____	_____	_____	☐
7. _____	_____	_____	☐
8. _____	_____	_____	☐
9. _____	_____	_____	☐
10. _____	_____	_____	☐
11. _____	_____	_____	☐
12. _____	_____	_____	☐
13. _____	_____	_____	☐
14. _____	_____	_____	☐

EVENING CHECKLIST

Morning Tasks　　　　　Mon　Tues　Wed　Thurs　Fri

_____

_____

_____

_____

_____

_____

_____

read	listen to music	journal	recite affirmations	set goals	
evening drink	take a bath/ shower	unplug	clean up	pack bag	
lay out uniform	make lunch	homework	chores	laundry	
empty out lunch bag	feed pets	pick out clothes for the next day	charge devices	put on pajamas	
brush teeth	go to bathroom	take vitamins/ medications	double-check or set a wake-up alarm	go to sleep early	

Checklist SUGGESTIONS

ACTIVITY TRACKER

WERE YOU ACTIVE TODAY?

	S	M	T	W	TH	F	S
WEEK 1							
WEEK 2							
WEEK 3							
WEEK 4							

IF NOT, WHAT ARE YOU WAITING FOR? GET OUTSIDE AND PLAY!

SLEEP TRACKER

HOW MANY HOURS OF SLEEP DID YOU GET LAST NIGHT?

	S	M	T	W	TH	F	S
Week 1							
Week 2							
Week 3							
Week 4							

IN ORDER TO GET 8 HOURS OF SLEEP, I NEED TO GO TO SLEEP BY

THIS WEEK

FAVORITE ACTIVITY

FAVORITE THING I LEARNED

FAVORITE MEAL

LEAST FAVORITE THING

WEEKLY
GOALS

WHAT ARE YOU PUTTING EFFORT IN TO GET ACCOMPLISHED THIS WEEK?

_____
_____
_____
_____

WHAT IS YOUR AFFIMATION FOR THE WEEK?

_____

RISING CHECKLIST

Morning Tasks Mon Tues Wed Thurs Fri

_____

_____

_____

_____

_____

_____

_____

_____

Checklist SUGGESTIONS

wake up when alarm goes off	brush teeth	eat breakfast	make bed	get dressed
clean up	wash face	shoes/ jacket	put homework in backpack	brush hair
pack a lunch	feed the pet	clean out school folder	take vitamins/ medications	gather important school papers
clear dishes from breakfast	put pajamas in clothes hamper	make snack for school	double-check backpack	grab lunch and devices
use the bathroom	avoid technology	get school notes signed	hugs and kisses	turn off all the lights

WEEKLY CHORE TRACKER

WEEK OF _____

	M	T	W	T	F	S	S

	M	T	W	T	F	S	S

	M	T	W	T	F	S	S

Homework Tracker

Week:

Assignment	Time Spent	Due date	✓
1.			☐
2.			☐
3.			☐
4.			☐
5.			☐
6.			☐
7.			☐
8.			☐
9.			☐
10.			☐
11.			☐
12.			☐
13.			☐
14.			☐

HOMEWORK TRACKER

Week: _____

Assignment	Time Spent	Due date	✓
1. _____	_____	_____	☐
2. _____	_____	_____	☐
3. _____	_____	_____	☐
4. _____	_____	_____	☐
5. _____	_____	_____	☐
6. _____	_____	_____	☐
7. _____	_____	_____	☐
8. _____	_____	_____	☐
9. _____	_____	_____	☐
10. _____	_____	_____	☐
11. _____	_____	_____	☐
12. _____	_____	_____	☐
13. _____	_____	_____	☐
14. _____	_____	_____	☐

EVENING CHECKLIST

Morning Tasks   Mon   Tues   Wed   Thurs   Fri

_____

_____

_____

_____

_____

_____

_____

Checklist SUGGESTIONS

read	listen to music	journal	recite affirmations	set goals
evening drink	take a bath/ shower	unplug	clean up	pack bag
lay out uniform	make lunch	homework	chores	laundry
empty out lunch bag	feed pets	pick out clothes for the next day	charge devices	put on pajamas
brush teeth	go to bathroom	take vitamins/ medications	double-check or set a wake-up alarm	go to sleep early

ACTIVITY TRACKER

WERE YOU ACTIVE TODAY?

	S	M	T	W	TH	F	S
WEEK 1							
WEEK 2							
WEEK 3							
WEEK 4							

IF NOT, WHAT ARE YOU WAITING FOR? GET OUTSIDE AND PLAY!

SLEEP TRACKER

HOW MANY HOURS OF SLEEP DID YOU GET LAST NIGHT?

	S	M	T	W	TH	F	S
Week 1							
Week 2							
Week 3							
Week 4							

IN ORDER TO GET 8 HOURS OF SLEEP, I NEED TO GO TO SLEEP BY

THIS WEEK

FAVORITE ACTIVITY

FAVORITE THING I LEARNED

FAVORITE MEAL

LEAST FAVORITE THING

END OF THE MONTH RECAP

SMALL WINS

1. _____
2. _____
3. _____

BIG ACHIEVEMENTS

1. _____
2. _____
3. _____

HIGHLIGHTS

_____
_____
_____
_____

LESSONS I LEARNED

_____
_____
_____
_____

WHAT WORKED WELL FOR ME

_____
_____
_____
_____
_____
_____
_____

WHAT I'LL STOP DOING

_____
_____
_____
_____
_____
_____
_____

IMPROVEMENTS TO MAKE

_____
_____
_____
_____

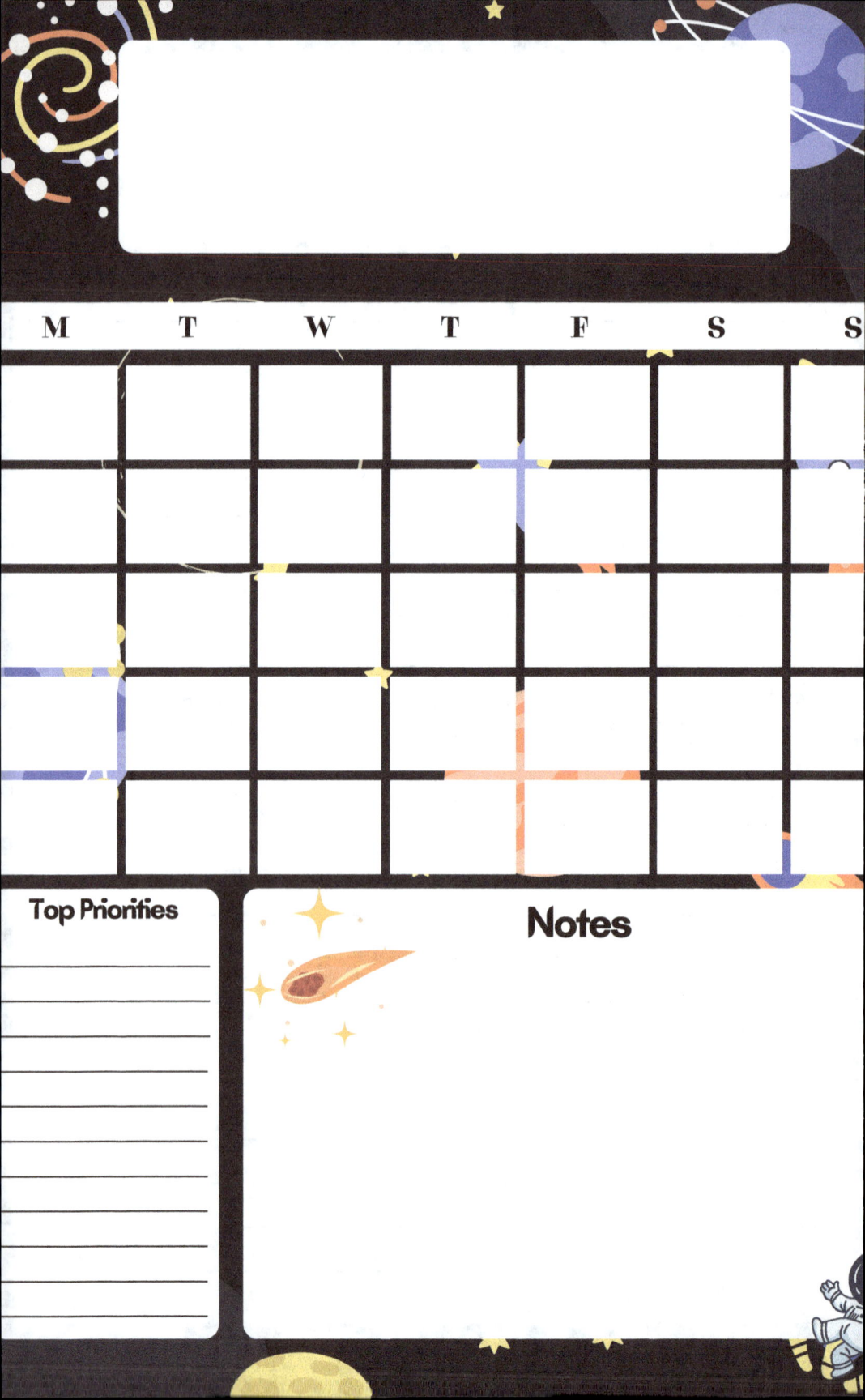

MONTHLY CHORE ASSIGNMENTS

What chores have your parents assigned you? (Grab a parent to help you fill out this page if you are not sure.)

DAILY CHORES

Kitchen
_____
_____
_____

Bathroom
_____
_____
_____

Living Room
_____
_____
_____

Bedroom
_____
_____
_____

WEEKLY CHORES

Kitchen
_____
_____
_____

Bathroom
_____
_____
_____

Living Room
_____
_____
_____

Bedroom
_____
_____
_____

EMOTIONS TRACKER

KEY

EVERY DAY FILL IN A SMALL PIECE OF THE PICTURE WITH THE COLOR LISTED FOR HOW YOU FELT TODAY

 HAPPY    EXCITED    WORRIED

 SAD    MAD    ANGRY

DAILY GRATITUDE LOG

WRITE DOWN 3 THINGS YOU ARE GRATEFUL FOR ON EACH LINE

1. ....
2. ....
3. ....
4. ....
5. ....
6. ....
7. ....
8. ....
9. ....
10. ....
11. ....
12. ....
13. ....
14. ....
15. ....
16. ....
17. ....
18. ....
19. ....
20. ....
21. ....
22. ....
23. ....
24. ....
25. ....
26. ....
27. ....
28. ....
29. ....
30. ....
31. ....

WEEKLY GOALS

WHAT ARE YOU PUTTING EFFORT IN TO GET ACCOMPLISHED THIS WEEK?

_____

_____

_____

_____

WHAT IS YOUR AFFIMATION FOR THE WEEK?

_____

RISING CHECKLIST

Morning Tasks   Mon   Tues   Wed   Thurs   Fri

_____

_____

_____

_____

_____

_____

_____

Checklist SUGGESTIONS

wake up when alarm goes off	brush teeth	eat breakfast	make bed	get dressed
clean up	wash face	shoes/ jacket	put homework in backpack	brush hair
pack a lunch	feed the pet	clean out school folder	take vitamins/ medications	gather important school papers
clear dishes from breakfast	put pajamas in clothes hamper	make snack for school	double-check backpack	grab lunch and devices
use the bathroom	avoid technology	get school notes signed	hugs and kisses	turn off all the lights

WEEKLY CHORE TRACKER

WEEK OF _____

	M	T	W	T	F	S	S

	M	T	W	T	F	S	S

	M	T	W	T	F	S	S

HOMEWORK TRACKER

Week: _____

Assignment	Time Spent	Due date	✓
1. _____	_____	_____	☐
2. _____	_____	_____	☐
3. _____	_____	_____	☐
4. _____	_____	_____	☐
5. _____	_____	_____	☐
6. _____	_____	_____	☐
7. _____	_____	_____	☐
8. _____	_____	_____	☐
9. _____	_____	_____	☐
10. _____	_____	_____	☐
11. _____	_____	_____	☐
12. _____	_____	_____	☐
13. _____	_____	_____	☐
14. _____	_____	_____	☐

Homework Tracker

Week:

Assignment	Time Spent	Due date	✓
1. _____	_____	_____	☐
2. _____	_____	_____	☐
3. _____	_____	_____	☐
4. _____	_____	_____	☐
5. _____	_____	_____	☐
6. _____	_____	_____	☐
7. _____	_____	_____	☐
8. _____	_____	_____	☐
9. _____	_____	_____	☐
10. _____	_____	_____	☐
11. _____	_____	_____	☐
12. _____	_____	_____	☐
13. _____	_____	_____	☐
14. _____	_____	_____	☐

EVENING CHECKLIST

Morning Tasks   Mon   Tues   Wed   Thurs   Fri

_____

_____

_____

_____

_____

_____

_____

_____

Checklist SUGGESTIONS

read	listen to music	journal	recite affirmations	set goals
evening drink	take a bath/ shower	unplug	clean up	pack bag
lay out uniform	make lunch	homework	chores	laundry
empty out lunch bag	feed pets	pick up clothes for the next day	charge devices	put on pajamas
brush teeth	go to bathroom	take vitamins/ medications	double-check or set a wake-up alarm	go to sleep early

ACTIVITY TRACKER

WERE YOU ACTIVE TODAY?

	S	M	T	W	TH	F	S
WEEK 1							
WEEK 2							
WEEK 3							
WEEK 4							

IF NOT, WHAT ARE YOU WAITING FOR? GET OUTSIDE AND PLAY!

SLEEP TRACKER

HOW MANY HOURS OF SLEEP DID YOU GET LAST NIGHT?

	S	M	T	W	TH	F	S
Week 1							
Week 2							
Week 3							
Week 4							

IN ORDER TO GET 8 HOURS OF SLEEP, I NEED TO GO TO SLEEP BY

THIS WEEK

FAVORITE ACTIVITY

FAVORITE THING I LEARNED

FAVORITE MEAL

LEAST FAVORITE THING

WEEKLY GOALS

WHAT ARE YOU PUTTING EFFORT IN TO GET ACCOMPLISHED THIS WEEK?

_____

_____

_____

_____

WHAT IS YOUR AFFIMATION FOR THE WEEK?

_____

RISING CHECKLIST

Morning Tasks   Mon   Tues   Wed   Thurs   Fri

_____ ○ ○ ○ ○ ○

_____ ○ ○ ○ ○ ○

_____ ○ ○ ○ ○ ○

_____ ○ ○ ○ ○ ○

_____ ○ ○ ○ ○ ○

_____ ○ ○ ○ ○ ○

_____ ○ ○ ○ ○ ○

_____ ○ ○ ○ ○ ○

Checklist SUGGESTIONS

wake up when alarm goes off	brush teeth	eat breakfast	make bed	get dressed
clean up	wash face	shoes/ jacket	put homework in backpack	brush hair
pack a lunch	feed the pet	clean out school folder	take vitamins/ medications	gather important school papers
clear dishes from breakfast	put pajamas in clothes hamper	make snack for school	double-check backpack	grab lunch and devices
use the bathroom	avoid technology	get school notes signed	hugs and kisses	turn off all the lights

WEEKLY CHORE TRACKER

WEEK OF _____

	M	T	W	T	F	S	S

	M	T	W	T	F	S	S

	M	T	W	T	F	S	S

HOMEWORK TRACKER

Week: _____

Assignment	Time Spent	Due date	✓
1. _____	_____	_____	☐
2. _____	_____	_____	☐
3. _____	_____	_____	☐
4. _____	_____	_____	☐
5. _____	_____	_____	☐
6. _____	_____	_____	☐
7. _____	_____	_____	☐
8. _____	_____	_____	☐
9. _____	_____	_____	☐
10. _____	_____	_____	☐
11. _____	_____	_____	☐
12. _____	_____	_____	☐
13. _____	_____	_____	☐
14. _____	_____	_____	☐

Homework Tracker

Week: _____

Assignment	Time Spent	Due date	✓
1. _____	_____	_____	☐
2. _____	_____	_____	☐
3. _____	_____	_____	☐
4. _____	_____	_____	☐
5. _____	_____	_____	☐
6. _____	_____	_____	☐
7. _____	_____	_____	☐
8. _____	_____	_____	☐
9. _____	_____	_____	☐
10. _____	_____	_____	☐
11. _____	_____	_____	☐
12. _____	_____	_____	☐
13. _____	_____	_____	☐
14. _____	_____	_____	☐

EVENING CHECKLIST

Morning Tasks | Mon | Tues | Wed | Thurs | Fri

read	listen to music	journal	recite affirmations	set goals
evening drink	take a bath/ shower	unplug	clean up	pack bag
lay out uniform	make lunch	homework	chores	laundry
empty out lunch bag	feed pets	pick out clothes for the next day	charge devices	put on pajamas
brush teeth	go to bathroom	take vitamins/ medications	double-check or set a wake-up alarm	go to sleep early

Checklist SUGGESTIONS

ACTIVITY TRACKER

WERE YOU ACTIVE TODAY?

	S	M	T	W	TH	F	S
WEEK 1							
WEEK 2							
WEEK 3							
WEEK 4							

IF NOT, WHAT ARE YOU WAITING FOR? GET OUTSIDE AND PLAY!

SLEEP TRACKER

HOW MANY HOURS OF SLEEP DID YOU GET LAST NIGHT?

	S	M	T	W	TH	F	S
Week 1							
Week 2							
Week 3							
Week 4							

IN ORDER TO GET 8 HOURS OF SLEEP, I NEED TO GO TO SLEEP BY

THIS WEEK

FAVORITE ACTIVITY

FAVORITE THING I LEARNED

FAVORITE MEAL

LEAST FAVORITE THING

WEEKLY GOALS

WHAT ARE YOU PUTTING EFFORT IN TO GET ACCOMPLISHED THIS WEEK?

_____

_____

_____

_____

WHAT IS YOUR AFFIMATION FOR THE WEEK?

_____

RISING CHECKLIST

Morning Tasks Mon Tues Wed Thurs Fri

_____

_____

_____

_____

_____

_____

_____

_____

Checklist SUGGESTIONS

wake up when alarm goes off	brush teeth	eat breakfast	make bed	get dressed
clean up	wash face	shoes/ jacket	put homework in backpack	brush hair
pack a lunch	feed the pet	clean out school folder	take vitamins/ medications	gather important school papers
clear dishes from breakfast	put pajamas in clothes hamper	make snack for school	double-check backpack	grab lunch and devices
use the bathroom	avoid technology	get school notes signed	hugs and kisses	turn off all the lights

WEEKLY CHORE TRACKER

WEEK OF _____

	M	T	W	T	F	S	S

	M	T	W	T	F	S	S

	M	T	W	T	F	S	S

HOMEWORK TRACKER

Week: _____

Assignment	Time Spent	Due date	✓
1. _____	_____	_____	☐
2. _____	_____	_____	☐
3. _____	_____	_____	☐
4. _____	_____	_____	☐
5. _____	_____	_____	☐
6. _____	_____	_____	☐
7. _____	_____	_____	☐
8. _____	_____	_____	☐
9. _____	_____	_____	☐
10. _____	_____	_____	☐
11. _____	_____	_____	☐
12. _____	_____	_____	☐
13. _____	_____	_____	☐
14. _____	_____	_____	☐

Homework Tracker

Week: _____

Assignment	Time Spent	Due date	✓
1. _____	_____	_____	☐
2. _____	_____	_____	☐
3. _____	_____	_____	☐
4. _____	_____	_____	☐
5. _____	_____	_____	☐
6. _____	_____	_____	☐
7. _____	_____	_____	☐
8. _____	_____	_____	☐
9. _____	_____	_____	☐
10. _____	_____	_____	☐
11. _____	_____	_____	☐
12. _____	_____	_____	☐
13. _____	_____	_____	☐
14. _____	_____	_____	☐

EVENING CHECKLIST

Morning Tasks   Mon   Tues   Wed   Thurs   Fri

_____   ○   ○   ○   ○   ○
_____   ○   ○   ○   ○   ○
_____   ○   ○   ○   ○   ○
_____   ○   ○   ○   ○   ○
_____   ○   ○   ○   ○   ○
_____   ○   ○   ○   ○   ○
_____   ○   ○   ○   ○   ○

Checklist SUGGESTIONS

read	listen to music	journal	recite affirmations	set goals
evening drink	take a bath/ shower	unplug	clean up	pack bag
lay out uniform	make lunch	homework	chores	laundry
empty out lunch bag	feed pets	pick out clothes for the next day	charge devices	put on pajamas
brush teeth	go to bathroom	take vitamins/ medications	double-check or set a wake-up alarm	go to sleep early

ACTIVITY TRACKER

WERE YOU ACTIVE TODAY?

	S	M	T	W	TH	F	S
WEEK 1							
WEEK 2							
WEEK 3							
WEEK 4							

IF NOT, WHAT ARE YOU WAITING FOR? GET OUTSIDE AND PLAY!

SLEEP TRACKER

HOW MANY HOURS OF SLEEP DID YOU GET LAST NIGHT?

	S	M	T	W	TH	F	S
Week 1							
Week 2							
Week 3							
Week 4							

IN ORDER TO GET 8 HOURS OF SLEEP, I NEED TO GO TO SLEEP BY

THIS WEEK

FAVORITE ACTIVITY

FAVORITE THING I LEARNED

FAVORITE MEAL

LEAST FAVORITE THING

WEEKLY
GOALS

WHAT ARE YOU PUTTING EFFORT IN TO GET ACCOMPLISHED THIS WEEK?

_____
_____
_____
_____

WHAT IS YOUR AFFIMATION FOR THE WEEK?

_____

RISING CHECKLIST

Morning Tasks   Mon   Tues   Wed   Thurs   Fri

_____

_____

_____

_____

_____

_____

_____

wake up when alarm goes off	brush teeth	eat breakfast	make bed	get dressed
clean up	wash face	shoes/ jacket	put homework in backpack	brush hair
pack a lunch	feed the pet	clean out school folder	take vitamins/ medications	gather important school papers
clear dishes from breakfast	put pajamas in clothes hamper	make snack for school	double-check backpack	grab lunch and devices
use the bathroom	avoid technology	get school notes signed	hugs and kisses	turn off all the lights

Checklist SUGGESTIONS

WEEKLY CHORE TRACKER

WEEK OF _____

	M	T	W	T	F	S	S

	M	T	W	T	F	S	S

	M	T	W	T	F	S	S

HOMEWORK TRACKER

Week: _____

Assignment	Time Spent	Due date	✓
1. _____	_____	_____	☐
2. _____	_____	_____	☐
3. _____	_____	_____	☐
4. _____	_____	_____	☐
5. _____	_____	_____	☐
6. _____	_____	_____	☐
7. _____	_____	_____	☐
8. _____	_____	_____	☐
9. _____	_____	_____	☐
10. _____	_____	_____	☐
11. _____	_____	_____	☐
12. _____	_____	_____	☐
13. _____	_____	_____	☐
14. _____	_____	_____	☐

Homework Tracker

Week: _____

Assignment	Time Spent	Due date	✓
1. _____	_____	_____	☐
2. _____	_____	_____	☐
3. _____	_____	_____	☐
4. _____	_____	_____	☐
5. _____	_____	_____	☐
6. _____	_____	_____	☐
7. _____	_____	_____	☐
8. _____	_____	_____	☐
9. _____	_____	_____	☐
10. _____	_____	_____	☐
11. _____	_____	_____	☐
12. _____	_____	_____	☐
13. _____	_____	_____	☐
14. _____	_____	_____	☐

EVENING CHECKLIST

Morning Tasks   Mon   Tues   Wed   Thurs   Fri

_____

_____

_____

_____

_____

_____

_____

_____

Checklist SUGGESTIONS

read	listen to music	journal	recite affirmations	set goals
evening drink	take a bath/ shower	unplug	clean up	pack bag
lay out uniform	make lunch	homework	chores	laundry
empty out lunch bag	feed pets	pick out clothes for the next day	charge devices	put on pajamas
brush teeth	go to bathroom	take vitamins/ medications	double-check or set a wake-up alarm	go to sleep early

ACTIVITY TRACKER

WERE YOU ACTIVE TODAY?

	S	M	T	W	TH	F	S
WEEK 1							
WEEK 2							
WEEK 3							
WEEK 4							

IF NOT, WHAT ARE YOU WAITING FOR? GET OUTSIDE AND PLAY!

SLEEP TRACKER

HOW MANY HOURS OF SLEEP DID YOU GET LAST NIGHT?

	S	M	T	W	TH	F	S
Week 1							
Week 2							
Week 3							
Week 4							

IN ORDER TO GET 8 HOURS OF SLEEP, I NEED TO GO TO SLEEP BY

THIS WEEK

FAVORITE ACTIVITY

FAVORITE THING I LEARNED

FAVORITE MEAL

LEAST FAVORITE THING

END OF THE MONTH RECAP

SMALL WINS

1. _____
2. _____
3. _____

BIG ACHIEVEMENTS

1. _____
2. _____
3. _____

HIGHLIGHTS

_____
_____
_____
_____

LESSONS I LEARNED

_____
_____
_____
_____

WHAT WORKED WELL FOR ME

_____
_____
_____
_____
_____
_____

WHAT I'LL STOP DOING

_____
_____
_____
_____
_____
_____

IMPROVEMENTS TO MAKE

_____
_____
_____
_____

REFLECTION

FAVORITE PART OF THE JOURNAL

A PART OF THIS JOURNEY YOU WILL NEVER FORGET

IMPROVEMENTS YOU SEE IN YOURSELF

GOALS FOR MOVING FORWARD

Welcome to Leadership

CERTIFICATE

This certificate confirms that

....

has been awarded the title of

LEADER

- Has a high self esteem
- Accepts your authentic self
- Lives according to your beliefs
- Respects yourself and others
- Trusts your strength and skills
- Takes initiative

You are the master of your own universe

Date

THEMOODYPOOL

The Master of your own UNIverse Leadership Journal was inspired by the authors 4 nephews- Angel, Tyler, Tyson, and DJ. The birth of these special individuals has left an imprint in her soul. It takes a village to raise children and The Moody Pool is an offering from her family to yours.

Publisher of multiple works, her upcoming children's line holds a special place in her heart.

Facebook & Instagram:
@TheMoodyPool

Website:
TheMoodyPool.com

www.ingramcontent.com/pod-product-compliance
Lightning Source LLC
Chambersburg PA
CBHW080031130526
44590CB00042BA/818